Practicing the Application of Health Education Skills and Competencies

Bette B. Keyser, Ed.D., CHES
Illinois State University

Marilyn J. Morrow, Ph.D., CHES
Illinois State University

Kathleen Doyle, Ph.D., CHES
Eastern Illinois University

Roberta Ogletree, H.S.D., CHES
Southern Illinois University at Carbondale

Nancy P. Parsons, Ph.D., CHES
Western Illinois University

Jones and Bartlett Publishers
Sudbury, Massachusetts

Boston   London   Singapore

Editorial, Sales, and Customer Service Offices

Jones and Bartlett Publishers
40 Tall Pine Drive
Sudbury, MA 01776
info@jbpub.com
http://www.jbpub.com

Jones and Bartlett Publishers International
Barb House, Barb Mews
London W6 7PA
UK

ISBN: 0-7637-0533-0

Printed in the United States of America
00 99 98 97   10 9 8 7 6 5 4 3 2 1

Dedication

To our parents, who first encouraged our love of teaching and learning

Genevieve & William Benewich
Helen & Charles Morrow
Annarae & Jack Phillips
Nadine & Sam Ogletree
Joan & Jack Parsons

and

To our students, who encourage us each day.

Acknowledgments

The authors wish to thank the following people who made this effort possible.

Janelle Hegrenes, this would not have happened without her.
Kelli McCormack Brown, for support and encouragement.
Jennifer LeGros, who typed the original proposal.
Eastern Illinois University students (HST 4250), who piloted many
    of the activities.
Bridget Kovach, Janelle Hegrenes, Sarah Schubert, and Donna Smith, from Illinois
        State University, who submitted work that is included.
Southern Illinois University at Carbondale students (HED 305 and HED 510),
        who piloted many of the activities.

Table of Contents

Chapter 4   **Evaluating the Effectiveness of Health Education Programs**

C. Interpret results of program evaluation.

D. Infer implications from findings for future program planning.

Chapter 5   **Coordinating Provision of Health Education Services**

A. Develop a plan for coordinating health education services.

Chapter 6   **Acting as a Resource Person in Health Education**

A. Utilized computerized health information systems effectively.

B. Establish effective consultative relationships with those requesting assistance in solving health-related problems.

Foreword

A primary goal of higher education is to prepare responsible individuals who will help advance the nation into the 21st century. In the best of worlds, these individuals will be characterized as critical thinkers, reflective practitioners, and sensitive and skilled communicators who also are technologically competent. We invite the reader to use this manual as one mechanism to help tomorrow's health educators meet this goal.

"Nothing in science has any value to society if it is not communicated."

Ann Rowe
American psychologist and author

This manual fills a need within the health education profession to apply and to communicate the roles, responsibilities, and competencies for entry level health educators in all practice settings. This manual primarily is written for new professionals; however, it also serves as a resource for professionals from all levels of experience. This manual represents a culmination of many other events—the Role Delineation Project, conferences at Birmingham and Bethesda, draft documents of the curriculum framework, and more. These events also share an evolutionary history and a common goal–to enhance the health and well-being of the individual, community, and society.

Identifying and delineating who we are and what we do has long been a challenge for the health education profession. Attendees at professional association meetings and professional preparation conferences from Jackson's Mill Conference in 1948 through the first Bethesda Conference in 1978 have addressed the most basic questions put forth to a profession, "Who are you? What do you do? What do you need to know to effectively do your job?"

The profession owes a debt of gratitude to the efforts and work accomplished by members of the National Task Force on the Preparation and Practice of Health Educators and later implemented by the National Commission for Health Education Credentialing. The vision, determination, and coordination efforts of these two groups provided the profession with landmark documents delineating the seven areas of responsibility for entry level health educators. Within each area of responsibility, terminal competencies (the main goals of instruction) as well as the enabling subcompetencies, which need to be mastered for task completion, are listed. This framework serves as the basis for the national, voluntary certification examination for health education specialists (the C.H.E.S. exam). Also, it is these responsibilities and competencies which form the basis of this manual. Even for the health educator who does not subscribe to the value of a certification credential, this manual serves as a key resource guide and organization roadmap for applying these competencies.

The authors are professionally prepared health educators with academic and professional experiences that cut across all practice settings. Additionally, the authors are teaching in professional preparation programs for health educators and are well versed in sound pedagogical techniques. These authors truly are practitioners as well as academicians. As a result, this manual has both an emphasis on foundational content and knowledge base, as well as an emphasis on skills development. Although process-oriented, the manual is user-friendly and encompasses a range of potential activities. The authors' "writing styles" are clear and succinct.

By far the manual's most distinctive features are the "hands-on" and interactive approach, definitive content, clear directions, contemporary resources, and ample illustrations for mastering development of the entry level competencies. Subsequently, this provides the reader with a virtual connectivity from the classroom to the daily activities of the worksetting. Further, this allows future health educators to actualize their mastery of content and enhance their skills development while completing activities relevant to the generic role of health educators. This manual's format also provides the instructor with a focused strategy and comprehensive approach for bridging the gap between the classroom and the workplace.

In the words of one of television's leading talk show hosts and a humanitarian in her own right, Oprah Winfrey once stated, "I think that education is power. I think that being able to communicate with people is power. One of my main goals on the planet is to encourage people to empower themselves." In the spirit of Oprah Winfrey, as well as the

similar philosophy of empowerment leader, Paulo Freire, we invite you to explore the
strategies in this manual and become empowered in the roles and responsibilities of entry level
health educators.

Elaine M. Vitello, Ph.D., CHES
Southern Illinois University at Carbondale

Sheila M. Patterson, Ph.D., CHES
West Chester University

January 1997

To The Instructor

The primary purpose of *Practicing the Application of Health Education Skills and Competencies* is to assist you and your students in linking health education content to skills that are required in school and community settings. Many faculty are integrating more skill development into courses as the demand for highly skilled health educators, not just content experts, has emerged. Although most students understand the general skill areas of health education, such as needs assessment or evaluation, many do not realize the numerous, specific skills needed to develop these general skills. This book is designed to help your students "bridge the gap" between content and skill by utilizing their knowledge to make decisions or solve problems identified in the activities.

This book was not conceived or written to be a single text for any one professional course. Rather, the authors feel there is a lack of specific learning activities for students during their professional preparation programs. Faculty in a health education program can work together to integrate the activities throughout the curriculum; perhaps Chapter 1 can be used in the needs assessment course, while Chapter 2 may be incorporated into the methods course. Program faculty can develop a unique approach to including the activities in the book, thereby assuring that graduates of their programs develop the requisite skills needed in health education today.

As you examine this book, please notice the special features that are included:

- Table of Contents which lists the location of each activity and worksheet

- Seven chapters, each devoted to one of the seven primary responsibilities of a health educator

- Short overview of each responsibility, followed by examples of this responsibility as practiced in various health education settings

- Two activities with student outcomes for each of 79 subcompetencies

- Detailed student instructions on how to successfully complete each activity

- Numerous worksheets which help organize completion of the activity
- Getting Started which provides students with ideas and addresses of resource materials helpful in beginning the activity
- Glossary of defined terms for each chapter with each term italicized when first used in that chapter
- References that refer to sources used to write the overview

Although there are two activities for each subcompetency, the authors do not expect an instructor to use both, but rather select one activity based upon class time and class size. Most activities are developed for each student to complete individually; however, some can be completed in groups. The activities can be class assignments as written or modified by you depending upon individual or class need. Activities can be used as graded assignments or as activities to be completed for practice or to stimulate discussion.

Worksheets have been developed for many of the activities. All pages in the book are perforated so students can easily remove a worksheet. Some students may prefer to set up the worksheet on their own word processing package. Again, it is the instructor's choice to decide what will work best. Many of the activities and worksheets may result in a health education product that can be included in students' portfolios.

As health education professionals who have committed their professional lives to the preparation of community and school health educators, we believe there are too few resources to assist faculty in incorporating a skill-based approach to professional preparation. We hope *Practicing the Application of Health Education Skills and Competencies* will strengthen health education programs being modified to better meet the needs of students entering the job market now and in the coming century.

To The Student

The primary focus of *Practicing the Application of Health Education Skills and Competencies* is to provide you with opportunities to apply and practice the many health education skills you are learning in courses. The activities in this book cannot be completed within a single course, but probably will be incorporated throughout many professional courses. Upon completion of the activities, you will feel more confident in your ability to perform the many and varied responsibilities of a health educator in a variety of settings. In addition, you will be able to "document" these skills, as many activities require you to complete a worksheet or develop a final product. Some of the activities will be appropriate for you to include in a professional portfolio, an educational tool that many new graduates are finding beneficial in the job market.

As you examine this book, please notice the special features that are included:

- Table of Contents which lists the location of each activity and worksheet

- Seven chapters, each devoted to one of the seven primary responsibilities of a health educator

- Short overview of each responsibility, followed by examples of this responsibility as practiced in various health education settings

- Two activities with student outcomes for each of 79 subcompetencies

- Detailed instructions on how to successfully complete each activity

- Numerous worksheets which help organize completion of the activity

- Getting Started which provides ideas and addresses of resource materials that will be helpful in beginning the activity

- Glossary of defined terms for each chapter with each term italicized when first used in that chapter

- References that refer to sources used to write the overview

The authors of *Practicing the Application of Health Education Skills and Competencies* have over 80 years of combined experience, teaching community and school health education students. It is our hope that this book will provide you with the skill-based approach that is receiving an increased emphasis in the health education profession. We have worked with many students like yourself who are preparing for a rewarding career as a health educator, but who worry about finding a school or community health position and being competitive in today's job market. Based upon our experiences, we believe the practice provided by these activities will help you fully develop your skills and be successful as you enter the health education field. Best of luck.

1   *Assessing Individual and Community Needs for Health Education*

Before a successful health education program can be planned, a thorough investigation of the target group is necessary. The process of systematically collecting data and gathering health-related information about the individual or community is referred to as a *needs assessment* (National Task Force on Preparation and Practice of Health Educators, 1985). Conducting a needs assessment requires the ability to locate information and/or generate data such as: demographic background of the target group, such as age, gender, educational and income level; health behaviors, knowledge, and attitudes of individuals or groups; and resources and services available within the community (Butler, 1994; Timmreck, 1995). The planner must also be able to analyze the information gathered to successfully identify health problems and measure gaps between services and *needs* of the target population (Windsor, Baranowski, Clark, & Cutter, 1984). This process has also been referred to as *community diagnosis* (Green, Kreuter, Deeds, & Partridge, 1980) and *community analysis* (Dignan & Carr, 1992). In the following paragraphs, specific examples will be provided to demonstrate how a needs assessment could be done to develop health education programs in different settings.

Community Health Setting

A *key informant* approach is used by the health educator to determine the receptivity, attitudes, and opinions of the community to a proposed adolescent pregnancy prevention program. Opinion leaders from the political, religious, educational, and medical groups within the community provide useful planning information and data for the health educator that could eventually increase the likelihood of the program's success and effectiveness.

Medical Setting

The health educator in planning a hospital-based hypertension program desires to focus on a specific aspect or variable of the condition. First, a *valid* and *reliable* instrument needs to be developed to survey a *representative sample* of the target group. The health educator then classifies health-related data according to specified variables such as age, gender, compliance factors, type of medication taken, etc. Data will be interpreted to determine the priority area or focus of the health education program.

Post-Secondary Setting

A *focus group* can be employed to assist the health educator who is planning a health promotion program for minority students attending a university. The focus group can be composed of student leaders from established minority associations, minority faculty members, and minority students from the general student population. Insight about specific health issues, health-related concerns, obstacles to treatment and/or health care, and the availability of resources on campus is useful information in determining the most important needs as perceived by the target group.

School Setting

In the development of comprehensive school health, the *scope* and *sequence* of the curriculum should be reflective of the social and cultural environments, growth and development factors, needs, and interests of the students. Thus, the health educator performs a *review of the literature* or accesses *computerized databases,* such as ERIC or PsycLIT, to obtain valid information about the developmental stages of the target group to develop the curriculum.

Worksite Setting

An unusually high absenteeism rate due to illnesses in a worksite prompts a health educator to conduct a needs assessment to determine what behaviors of the employees foster well-being and which hinder it. Using a *health-risk appraisal* as a tool, the health educator gathers health histories and health behaviors of the target group to plan individual or group health education programs that address specific risk factors.

The activities on the following pages provide opportunities to experiment with a variety of needs assessment methods that can be used to investigate a target group or collect health-related data about the individual or community. The activities have been designed to provide the student with opportunities to develop skills in many aspects of a health education needs assessment.

Assessing Individual and Community Needs for Health Education

Competency A
Obtain health-related data about social and cultural environments, growth and development factors, needs, and interests.

Sub-Competency 1
Select valid sources of information about health needs and information.

<u>Activity: Ethnic/Racial Diversity In Health Needs And Interests</u>

Student Outcome: The student can identify health-specific publications and resource articles related to social/cultural influences on health needs/interests of different racial/ethnic groups.

Directions:

1.   Research the following groups of people:
        * African Americans
        * Native Americans
        * Asian Americans
        * Hispanics
        * Pacific Islanders

2.   Use the chart on the following page as a guide to information to be researched and recorded.

3.   Refer to a variety of sources for the needed information.

4.   Discuss:

        * Differences and similarities in health needs of the groups.
        * Differences and similarities in health interests of the groups.
        * How membership in racial or ethnic groups may impact health needs and interests.

<u>Getting Started</u>

Contact in writing or by phone: Office of Minority Health Resource Center, PO Box 37337, Washington, DC 20013-7337, 1-800-444-6472

OR

check the Web site: http://www.omhrc.gov

RACIAL/ETHNIC DIVERSITY IN HEALTH NEEDS AND INTERESTS

Health Needs/Interests	Social/Cultural Beliefs/Values Influencing Health Needs and Interests	Sources of Information
AFRICAN AMERICANS		
1.		
2.		
3.		
4.		
5.		
NATIVE AMERICANS		
1.		
2.		
3.		
4.		
5.		
ASIAN AMERICANS		
1.		
2.		
3.		
4.		
5.		

RACIAL/ETHNIC DIVERSITY IN HEALTH NEEDS AND INTERESTS (cont.)

Health Needs/Interests	Social/Cultural Beliefs/Values Influencing Health Needs and Interests	Sources of Information
HISPANICS		
1.		
2.		
3.		
4.		
5.		
PACIFIC ISLANDERS		
1.		
2.		
3.		
4.		
5.		

Assessing Individual and Community Needs for Health Education

Competency A
Obtain health-related data about social and cultural environments, growth and development factors, needs, and interests.

Sub-Competency 1
Select valid sources of information about health needs and information.

Activity: Evaluating National Health Surveys

Student Outcome: The student can identify articles that describe two well known health *surveys*. In addition, the student can identify similarities and differences between the two instruments and evaluate each as a valid tool for gathering data.

Directions:

1.   Locate and read one journal article that describes use of the NASHS (National Adolescent Student Health Survey) and one that describes use of the YRBS (Youth Risk Behavior Survey).

2.   Develop a short paper comparing and contrasting these two survey instruments. In particular, address the following issues:

   * What background information from the journal reading did you find about the development of the NASHS and YRBS?
   * What does each survey assess? Knowledge, attitudes, behaviors?
   * What type of questions are on each? (For example, multiple choice, fill in the blank, etc.)
   * Are there questions that might be considered controversial and require approval before administration? Explain.
   * Do you consider each a valid source of information? Justify why or why not.
   * List the two journal references utilized for this paper.

Getting Started

American School Health Association, Association for the Advancement of Health Education, Society for Public Health Education, Inc. (1989). The national adolescent student health survey: A report on the health of America's youth. Oakland, CA: Third Party Publishing.

Centers for Disease Control and Prevention. (1993). Youth risk behavior surveillance - United States, 1993. Morbidity and Mortality Weekly Report. 44 (No. SS-1).

Assessing Individual and Community Needs for Health Education

Competency A
Obtain health-related data about social and cultural environments, growth and development factors, needs, and interests.

Sub-Competency 1
Select valid sources of information about health needs and information.

Activity: Growth And Development, Health Needs, And Health Interests According To Age Group

Student Outcome: The student can identify valid sources to consult when needing information about health needs and interests according to age.

Directions:

1.   Select one age group about which you wish to know more (i.e., preschool, elementary, adolescence, middle age, elderly adults).

2.   Identify several valid sources that provide information about the growth and development characteristics, health needs, and health interests of the selected age group.

3.   State information found for age group on the chart provided.

4.   Provide reference information on sources used. What criteria did you use to decide each source was valid?

Getting Started

Creswell, W. H., Jr., & Newman, I. M. (1993). School health practice (10th ed.). St. Louis: Mosby-Year Book.

Foder, J. T., Dalis, G. T., & Giarratano, S. C. (1995). Health instruction: Theory and application (5th ed.). Philadelphia: Lea and Febiger.

Also, conduct on-line database searches for sources that focus on human growth and development, survey findings of health needs and/or interests of a specific age group, or national studies on health interests.

Growth and Development, Health Needs, and
Health Interests According to Age Group

Age Group: _____

Growth and Development Characteristics:

Source(s):

Health Needs:

Source(s):

Health Interests:

Source(s):

Define limits of age group:

_____

_____

Reference(s) used to define age group:

_____

_____

_____

Notes

Assessing Individual and Community Needs for Health Education

Competency A
Obtain health-related data about social and cultural environments, growth and development factors, needs, and interests.

Sub-Competency 2
Utilize computerized sources of health-related information.

Activity: Office Of Minority Health Resource Center Database

Student Outcome: The student can access one of six databases available through the Office of Minority Health including the minority health resource center database, the minority health funding database, the minority media database, the minority health research database, the minority health data resources database, and the resource persons network.

Directions:

1.   Select a specific health concern of a minority group.

2.   Call the Office of Minority Health, U.S. Public Health Service, Department of Health and Human Services.

3.   Request that the appropriate computer data base be accessed to search for information on the specific topic and specific minority group and that the resulting printout of information be sent to you.

4.   Examine and summarize the information you receive for the listing of sources.

5.   Submit the print-outs to the instructor.

Getting Started

U.S. Department of Health & Human Services, Public Health Service, Office of Minority Health, PO Box 37337, Washington, DC 20013-7337, 1-800-444-6472

OR

The Web site for the Office of Minority Health is: http://www.omhrc.gov

Assessing Individual and Community Needs for Health Education

Competency A
Obtain health-related data about social and cultural environments, growth and development factors, needs, and interests.

Sub-Competency 2
Utilize computerized sources of health-related information.

Activity: Surfing The Web

Student Outcome: The student can identify, utilize, and interact with *World Wide Web* sources to obtain health-related information.

Directions:

1.   "Surf the Web" by accessing *Internet*. Institutions may use different methods to access Internet. Gather information appropriate to your institution regarding how to access Internet and the World Wide Web (WWW).

2.   Some sources on the WWW provide information only with no interactive capabilities (i.e., bulletin board services, frequently asked questions [FAQs], etc.). Others involve interactive participation, either with individuals or discussion groups (i.e., e-mail, newsgroups, etc.).

3.   Access five sources which provide information only. Obtain information from each.

4.   Access two interactive sources of your choice and demonstrate participation in those discussions by printing your questions/comments and the responses you receive.

Getting Started

The following sources provide suggestions on where to start your search:

New Riders Publishing. (1996). New Riders' official world wide web yellow pages (summer/fall 1996 ed.). Indianapolis, IN: Author.

New Riders Publishing. (1996, August). Inside the world wide web (2nd ed.). Indianapolis, IN: Author.

World Wide Web *Uniform Resource Locators (URLs)*

Databases

http://cedr.lbl.gov/cdrom/lookup/	(1990 Census Lookup)
http://wwonder.cdc.gov/	(CDC Wonder)
http://www.nlm.nih.gov/	(HLM Online Databases and Databanks)

Government

http://www.cdc.gov/	(Centers for Disease Control and Prevention)
http://www.os.dhhs.gov/	(Department of Health and Human Services)
http://www.epa.gov/	(Environmental Protection Agency)
http://www.nih.gov/	(National Institutes of Health)
http://www.osha.gov/	(Occupational Safety and Health Administration)

Health-Related

http://www.columbia.edu/cu/healthwise/	(Go Ask Alice)
http://www.healthgate.com/	(HealthGate)
http://www.ihr.com/topics.html/	(Online Health Topics)
http://www.medscape.com/	(MedScape)
http://www.cc.emory.edu/WHSCL/medweb.html/	(MedWeb: Biomedical Internet Resources)

Notes

Assessing Individual and Community Needs for Health Education

Competency A
Obtain health-related data about social and cultural environments, growth and development factors, needs, and interests.

Sub-Competency 2
Utilize computerized sources of heath-related information.

Activity: Utilizing ERIC To Locate Health-Related Data

Student Outcome: The student can develop competence in using a computerized database to locate materials that are specific to health needs of racial/ethnic groups.

Directions:

1.   Identify a racial/ethnic group that you would like to learn more about. Refer to the ERIC Thesaurus to identify the correct descriptor.

2.   Select one of the following topic areas: Health Needs, Health Interests, Social Factors, or Cultural Factors. Using the ERIC Thesaurus, identify three descriptors that describe your selection.

3.   For each of the descriptors, copy the scope note (SN) and date when the term was first used. List at least one broader term (BT), a narrower term (NT), and 3 related terms (RT). Refer to the examples listed below.

4.   If any information is missing, write in MISSING. Do not leave blanks.

Examples of ERIC Information Needed

Term 1 (Racial/Ethnic Group) _____

Date First Used in ERIC _____

SN _____

BT _____   NT _____

RT _____   _____   _____

Term 2 (Topic Area) _____

Date First Used in ERIC _____

SN _____

BT _____ NT _____

RT _____ _____ _____

5.   Next use the computer to combine terms for the racial/ethnic group with the three
        descriptors chosen to describe health needs, health interests, social factors, or cultural
        factors. For example, combine "racial/ethnic group" with "health need."

6.   PRINT OUT the entries using the PRINT Command and attach the printout to this
        assignment sheet.

Getting Started

Houston, J. E. (1990). Thesaurus of ERIC descriptors (12th ed.). Phoenix, AR:
Oryx. (This is an alphabetical listing of terms used for indexing and searching in the ERIC
system. The thesaurus is usually placed near the computers that have ERIC.)

Assessing Individual and Community Needs for Health Education

Competency A
Obtain health-related data about social and cultural environments, growth and development factors, needs, and interests.

Sub-Competency 3
Employ or develop appropriate data-gathering information.

Activity: Development Of A Pretest For High School Students

Student Outcome: The student can design a multiple choice question pretest that is refined by receiving peer feedback.

Directions:

1.   Imagine that you are a public health educator who had been asked to present information about HIV/AIDS to a class of freshmen at the local high school. You will only be given two class periods so you decide to develop a pretest on HIV knowledge.

2.   The teacher has agreed to administer the test and provide the results to you a week before you visit the high school. You decide to write the questions in multiple choice format.

3.   Prior to the writing of questions, consult at least 2 sources (textbooks, American Red Cross materials, etc.) to determine the sequence/scope of HIV material suggested for high school students. You may wish to see if the materials suggested at the end of this exercise are available in the library.

4.   Develop a 15 question multiple choice pretest for freshmen students. Include the following information:

> * Title of the instrument
> * Directions to the students
> * A minimum of 15 multiple choice questions covering the important
>   information about HIV

5.   On the due date, bring five copies of your pretest.

6.   Within your group, provide feedback on each pretest as to clarity of direction and question construction.

7.   Following the peer critiques, participate in a class discussion on some of the strengths and weaknesses of the pretests and the types of revisions to be made.

8.   Incorporate suggestions from the peer critiques and submit the original and revised pretests to the instructor.

<u>Getting Started</u>

American Red Cross. (1990). <u>American Red Cross instructor candidate training participant's manual.</u> Washington, DC: Author.

Rathus, S. A., & Boughn, S. (1993). <u>AIDS: What every student needs to know</u> (2nd ed.). Fort Worth, TX: Harcourt Brace.

Seek additional resources for information regarding design of multiple choice questions.

Assessing Individual and Community Needs for Health Education

Competency A
Obtain health-related data about social and cultural environments, growth and development factors, needs, and interests.

Sub-Competency 3
Employ or develop appropriate data-gathering information.

Activity: Formal Needs Assessment Techniques

Student Outcome: The student can differentiate among five types of formal needs assessment techniques.

Directions:

1.   Locate the article cited under "Getting Started" for this activity.

2.   Complete the chart on the following page with the requested information on the five types of formal needs assessment techniques:

    * how the process works
    * use in health education
    * make up of the target population
    * special considerations

3.   Develop an example of appropriate use of each of the processes in health education needs assessment in various settings such as school, community, worksite, or medical.

Getting Started

Gilmore, G. D. (1977). Needs assessment processes for community health education. International Quarterly of Community Health Education, 20, 164-173.

Notes

FORMAL NEEDS ASSESSMENT TECHNIQUES

Assessment Technique	Process	Use	Target Population	Special Considerations
Delphi Process				
Nominal Group Process				
Advisory Committee				
Telephone Survey				
Creative Assessment				

Notes

Assessing Individual and Community Needs for Health Education

Competency A
Obtain health-related data about social and cultural environments, growth and development factors, needs, and interests.

Sub-Competency 4
Apply survey techniques to acquire health data.

Activity: Community Profile

Student Outcome: The student can learn to utilize census data to assess the health needs of a selected community.

Directions:

1.   Locate the most current state governmental population census documents in the library.

2.   Select a community in your home state or state in which you are currently residing that has sufficient governmental data to respond to the following Community Profile worksheet.

3.   Complete the Community Profile worksheet by finding the specific table in the cited government document (state), then entering the statistical data into the spaces provided.

4.   Review the Community Profile worksheet and identify any implications for health education programming in that specific community.

Getting Started

Obtain the two following government documents for your state:

    1.   1990 Census Population: General Population Characteristics
    2.   1990 Census Population: Social and Economic Characteristics

Note: Corrected Tables for some states were issued in July 1992 for the 1990 Census of Population and Housing: Summary of Social, Economic, and Housing Characteristics.

Notes

Community Profile of

_____

1990 Census of Population: General Population Characteristics

---

Table 1. Summary of General Characteristics of Persons

_____ 1990 Population (All persons)
_____ Under 5 years (Percent of all persons)
_____ Under 18 years
_____ 18 to 24 years
_____ 25 to 44 years
_____ 45-64 years
_____ 65 years and over
_____ 80 years and over

_____ Median Age

Table 2. Summary of General Characteristics of Households and Families

_____ Persons per household
_____ Persons per family

Table 6. Race and Hispanic Origin

Percent Distribution by Race
_____ White
_____ Black
_____ American Indian, Eskimo, or Aleut
_____ Asian or Pacific Islander
_____ Other Race
_____ Hispanic Origin (of any race)

1990 Census of Population: Social and Economic Characteristics

Table 1. Summary of Social Characteristics

_____ % Foreign Born
_____ % Who speak a language other than English at home
_____ % High school graduate or higher (25 years and over)
_____ % With bachelor's degree or higher (25 years and over)
_____ % Persons 16-19 not enrolled in school and not high school graduate

Table 2. Summary of Labor Force and Commuting Characteristics

_____ % Of persons 16 and over in labor force (total)
_____ % Of persons 16 and over in labor force (male)
_____ % Of persons 16 and over in labor force (female)
_____ % Of persons 16 and over in labor force (female with own children under 6 years)
_____ % Of persons 16 and over in labor force who use public transportation
_____ Mean travel time to work (minutes)

Table 3. Summary of Occupation, Income and Poverty Characteristics

_____ Median income in households in 1989 (dollars)
_____ Median income in families in 1989 (dollars)
_____ Percent of families below poverty level in 1989

Table 170. Fertility and Family Composition

_____ Persons per household
_____ Persons per family
_____ Female households, no husband present

Assessing Individual and Community Needs for Health Education

Competency A
Obtain health-related data about social and cultural environments, growth and development factors, needs, and interests.

Sub-Competency 4
Apply survey techniques to acquire health data.

Activity: Comparing Sets Of Data

Student Outcome: The student can collect data concerning a health issue and compare the results with similar data collected by a different source.

Prerequisite for Activity: Video, <u>Traits of a Healthy Family</u>, based on the work by Dolores Curran (see information at end of activity).

Directions:

1. Ask 10 of your college friends/acquaintances to identify three important traits of a healthy family.

2. Record responses by gender and on assigned day bring to class.

3. In small groups categorize similar responses. For example, "can talk to one another" could be grouped with "communicate well among family members." Tally the responses by gender. Share group findings orally with the rest of the class.

4. Submit group data to instructor who will compile data into graph format, first comparing the responses by gender, and second showing total responses of all respondents.

5. View the video in the next class period. Record the traits of the healthy family as expressed by Dolores Curran.

6. Following the video, view the graphs prepared by the instructor. Discuss similarities and differences between the student responses and information provided in the video. Project possible reasons for the differences.

Getting Started

"Traits of a Healthy Family," based on the work by Delores Curran. Harper Video Cassette, Harper and Row. ISBN 0-06-254819-0.

Assessing Individual and Community Needs for Health Education

Competency B
Distinguish between behaviors that foster and those that hinder well-being.

Sub-Competency 1
Investigate physical, social, emotional, and intellectual factors influencing health behaviors.

Activity: Health Behavior Influences

Student Outcome: The student can analyze health behavior according to a variety of influencing factors.

Directions:

1.   Select a health behavior and an appropriate target group. Examples:

* Unprotected sex and college students
* Smokeless tobacco use and teenagers
* Seat belt use and adults
* Lack of exercise and elderly individuals

2.   Conduct a library search to identify at least five articles that describe research on factors influencing the specific behavior.

3.   Based on the search, complete the following chart by first identifying the study by author and year. Second, list the specific factor influencing the health behavior by classifying it as either physical, social, emotional, or intellectual. For example, if the topic was smokeless tobacco use, a factor might be peer influence and is best classified as a social influence.

4.   After charting information from the five studies, write a summary of the studies and the identified factors. Include conclusions on which factors were identified in more than one study and which factors were cited only once. Attach a reference list of the articles reviewed for information.

Getting Started

Use computer databases such as PsycLIT to identify relevant articles. Be sure to use the thesaurus associated with the database, such as Thesaurus of Psychological Index Terms for PsycLIT and Thesaurus of ERIC Descriptors for ERIC. The former thesaurus uses "tobacco smoking" and "junior high school students," while the latter thesaurus uses "tobacco" and "early adolescents."

HEALTH BEHAVIOR INFLUENCES

Health Behavior _____   Target Population _____

Name of Study: 1:   2:   3:   4:   5:

Author/Year:

Factors:

Physical

Social

Emotional

Intellectual

Notes

Assessing Individual and Community Needs for Health Education

Competency B
Distinguish between behaviors that foster and those that hinder well-being.

Sub-Competency 1
Investigate physical, social, emotional, and intellectual factors influencing health behaviors.

Activity: Health Determinants Investigation

Student Outcome: The student can identify and describe how physical, social, emotional, intellectual, and environmental factors influence health behaviors.

Directions:

1.   List specific factors which influence health behaviors in each of the following categories: physical, social, emotional, intellectual, and environmental. One example of a social factor is poverty.

2.   Describe how each factor specifically influences health behavior.

3.   Compare and discuss your ideas with others.

Assessing Individual and Community Needs for Health Education

Competency B
Distinguish between behaviors that foster and those that hinder well-being.

Sub-Competency 2
Identify behaviors that tend to promote or compromise health.

<u>Activity</u>: <u>Behaviorism Exploration</u>

Student Outcome: The student can identify behaviors and describe how they positively or negatively affect health.

Directions:

1.   Brainstorm a list of five behaviors which tend to promote and five that compromise health. Record the behaviors in the proper column on the worksheet provided.

2.   For each health promoting behavior, describe how the behavior positively affects health. Similarly, describe how each health compromising behavior negatively affects health. Provide examples of how the behavior contributes to specific disorders and/or diseases. Record the responses in the appropriate column on the worksheet provided.

3.   Discuss the responses with others to obtain others' opinions/ideas. This may be done with others in class or outside of class.

BEHAVIORISM EXPLORATION

Directions: List the behaviors which promote (+) or compromise (-) health. Indicate how the behavior affects health by recording specific examples in the "Health Outcomes" column.

BEHAVIOR	+ OR -	HEALTH OUTCOMES

Notes

Assessing Individual and Community Needs for Health Education

Competency B
Distinguish between behaviors that foster and those that hinder well-being.

Sub-Competency 2
Identify behaviors that tend to promote or compromise health.

<u>Activity: Lifestyle Influences On Health</u>

Student Outcome: The student can identify and appraise lifestyle behaviors that promote or hinder health at various stages of the life cycle. Upon examining the lifestyle behaviors, the student will draw conclusions as to which behaviors have the greatest impact on the health of Americans.

Directions:

1.   Research the leading causes of morbidity and mortality for the following age groups:

          * infants (include maternal behaviors that influence fetal/infant health)
            children
          * adolescents
          * adults
          * older adults

2.   Identify specific behaviors that are known to promote health as well as behaviors known to compromise health for each group listed above. Enter this information onto the chart.

3.   Submit a two page paper to the instructor that draws relevant conclusions as to which lifestyle behaviors promote and compromise the overall health of Americans.

<u>Getting Started</u>

Conduct an on-line search for the information above using CDC Wonder, Yahoo Health, U.S. Department of Health & Human Services, or other health-related World Wide Web servers.

Notes

LIFESTYLE INFLUENCES ON HEALTH

	Promotes: Compromises:
Infants	
	Promotes: Compromises:
Children	
	Promotes: Compromises:
Adolescents	

LIFESTYLE INFLUENCES ON HEALTH (cont.)

Adults	Promotes:
	Compromises:
Older Adults	Promotes:
	Compromises:

Assessing Individual and Community Needs for Health Education

Competency B
Distinguish between behaviors that foster and those that hinder well-being.

Sub-Competency 3
Recognize the role of learning and affective experiences in shaping patterns
of health behavior.

Activity: Combating Competing Sources Of Health Information

Student Outcome: The student can recognize that there are sources of health information and influences on attitudes and behavior that are not a part of planned health instruction.

Directions:

1.   Identify three possible sources of health information for an elementary school aged child other than school health instruction.

2.   For each source identified, list a specific experience an elementary school aged child might have that could impact negatively his/her health attitudes and behavior.

3.   Provide a suggestion or teaching idea that the health instructor could utilize to deal with these competing sources of health information.

Getting Started

Interview elementary school teachers, nurses, and/or administrators for their opinions on the above questions.

Assessing Individual and Community Needs for Health Education

Competency B
Distinguish between behaviors that foster and those that hinder well-being.

Sub-Competency 3
Recognize the role of learning and affective experiences in shaping patterns
of health behavior.

<u>Activity: <u>What's Your Preference: Head Or Heart?</u></u>

Student Outcome: The student can be sensitive to individuals who prefer learning experiences
that are primarily cognitive or primarily affective.

Directions:

1.   Each student will find a statistic or fact about the influence of alcohol on individuals
        and society.

2.   In class, the instructor will go around the room and write each statistic or fact on the
        board.

3.   Within a circle, each student will be asked to share, if comfortable, an experience in
        which alcohol has affected his or her life or someone s/he knows.

4.   When sharing is completed, students will discuss their opinions on how they feel
        about the learning value of the presented factual material vs. the learning value of
        listening to another student describe experiences related to alcohol.

<u>Getting Started</u>

National Safety Council. (1995). <u>Accident facts</u> (1995 ed.). Itasca, IL: Author.

Assessing Individual and Community Needs for Health Education

Competency C
Infer needs for health education on the basis of obtained data.

Sub-Competency 1
Examine needs assessment data.

Activity: Analyzing Data From A HIV Pretest For High School Students

Student Outcome: The student can interpret data gathered through a questionnaire.

Directions:

1.   Refer to the pretest developed in the activity, "Development of a Pretest for High School Students" (p. 17).

2.   Make copies of the questionnaire and ask at least 15 individuals to complete the pretest.

3.   Use a simple computer spreadsheet program such as Lotus, Excel, or Quattro (or compute by hand) to obtain *descriptive statistics* and complete the chart below.

Number of Subjects	
Mean Score	
Median Score	
Standard Deviation	

4.   Based upon the results, write a sentence or two describing the knowledge of the target group concerning HIV.

Getting Started

Consult any basic statistics book for information on how to compute descriptive statistics.

Phillips, D. (1978). Basic statistics for health sciences. San Francisco: W. H. Freeman.

Sarvela, P. D., & McDermott, R. J. (1993). Health education evaluation and measurement: A practitioner's perspective. Madison, WI: Brown and Benchmark.

Assessing Individual and Community Needs for Health Education

Competency C
Infer needs for health education on the basis of obtained data.

Sub-Competency 1
Examine needs assessment data.

<u>Activity</u>: <u>The ABCs Needs Assessment Interview</u>

Student Outcome: The student can cite specific data obtained by an agency and how it is analyzed for determining needs or health education.

Directions:

1.   Select a local or state agency or organization, such as the local public health department, American Lung Association, Planned Parenthood, and Mothers Against Drunk Driving (MADD), for conducting an on-site interview.

2.   Contact agency to request an appointment to interview appropriate personnel on the process of obtaining and analyzing needs assessment data for health education.

3.   Use the following 10 questions to guide you during the interview:

   a. What is the mission of the agency or organization?
   b. How often does the agency determine need for new programs or modifications of existing health education programs?
   c. Are data used to justify potential decisions regarding health education?
   d. If so, what types of data are gathered for use in making decisions for programmatic additions or changes?
   e. Why are the specific data chosen to be gathered and used?
   f. Who is responsible for gathering the data?
   g. How are the data analyzed?
   h. Who receives the analysis of data?
   i. What format is used to present the data to others?
   j. How long does the whole process take to identify, collect, and analyze appropriate data, then display it in a format for others to understand?

4.   Share findings with classmates. Compare and contrast types of data used for needs assessment, means for gathering, analyzing and interpreting data for decision makers, and time frames for needs assessment data gathering and analysis process.

5.   Write a thank you letter to the interviewee indicating your appreciation for the information and its usefulness in understanding the needs assessment process.

Assessing Individual and Community Needs for Health Education

Competency C
Infer needs for health education on the basis of obtained data.

Sub-Competency 2
Determine priority areas of need for health education.

Activity: Decision-Making Models

Student Outcome: The student can identify two types of decision-making models that can be used to prioritize health education needs.

Directions:

1.   Locate some of the sources listed under "Getting Started" in this section.

2.   From the readings, select two different decision-making models.

3.   Complete the chart on the next page with the names of the models selected and key information about each.

Getting Started

Rowe, A., Mason, R., Dickel, K., & Snyder, N. (1989). Strategic management. Reading, MA: Addison-Wesley.

Spiegel, A., & Hyman, H. (1978). Basic health planning methods. Rockville, MD: Aspen.

Timmreck, T. C. (1995). Planning, program development, and evaluation: A handbook for health promotion, aging, and health services. Boston: Jones and Bartlett.

Notes

DECISION-MAKING MODELS

	Model Name:	Model Name:
Purpose		
Key Components		
Key Information Needed		

Notes

Assessing Individual and Community Needs for Health Education

Competency C
Infer needs for health education on the basis of obtained data.

Sub-Competency 2
Determine priority areas of need for health education.

Activity: Determining Priority Areas For Health Education

Student Outcome: The student can compare and contrast sources of data for determining priority areas for health education.

Directions:

1. In groups of three or four students, select an age group, such as infants, teenagers, or elderly, or a specific minority population. Then brainstorm to identify a variety of sources that may provide information relevant to that population when determining priority areas for health education. For example, priority areas for adolescent health education may be determined by examining information and data generated at different levels:

National:	Healthy People 2000 Publications Youth Risk Behavior Survey National Health Education Standards
State:	Legislation on School Health Education Student Knowledge, Attitude, Belief, Behavior Surveys State Public Health Department
Local:	Law Enforcement Agency Local Public Health Department Mothers Against Drunk Drinking (MADD) Planned Parenthood Agency Junior/Senior High School Health Educators, School Nurses, and Curriculum Advisory Groups

    *Note: It is helpful if the groups select different target areas, which improves access to the resources needed.

2. Each member of the group should locate data from one of the sources and bring it to the next class. Complete the attached chart as a group.

3. Analyze chart findings to determine similarities and differences in identification of priority areas for health education.

4. Summarize findings of analysis in writing and submit to instructor along with the chart.

Notes

DETERMINING PRIORITY AREAS FOR HEALTH EDUCATION

Title of Document	Date of Publication	Source of Resource (Where was it Located?)	Major Priority Areas Based on Findings

Notes

Glossary of Terms

community analysis: collection of data and information about a community's backdrop, health status, health care system, and social assistance system

community diagnosis: synthesis of data collected during the community analysis with the purpose of identifying gaps in health status and health services

computerized databases: collections of journals, pamphlets, books, reports, or audiovisual materials loaded onto computer systems

delphi process: a technique whereby experts are consulted and arrive at consensus about planning or solving a problem

descriptive statistics: the use of statistics to summarize data; frequency counts, mean, median, mode, standard deviation

focus group: a needs assessment strategy in which a small group of individuals (6 to 12) are moderated during a discussion about a selected issue in order to obtain opinions, beliefs, and attitudes toward that issue

health-risk appraisal: an instrument that compares data about an individual's health history and behavior to a data base that contains information from individuals of the same gender, race, and age

Internet: the world's largest computer network; the "net" is a network of networks, all freely exchanging information; it links approximately 25 to 30 million people on 35,000 different networks

key informant: formal or informal knowledgeable leaders in community

need: something required or desired that is lacking

needs assessment: collecting data and information about a target group for the purpose of determining priority areas for health education programs

nominal group process: a structured meeting that involves an orderly procedure for obtaining information from target population groups who are closely associated with a specific problem

reliable: an instrument will be consistent in the measuring process each time it is used

representative sample: participants selected for the study accurately reflect the knowledge, attitudes, and behavior of the population

review of the literature: a systematic inspection and examination of the recorded information on a specific topic

scope: the range of health topics to be included in a curriculum or program

sequence: the order or arrangement of topics/subject matter in a curriculum or program

survey: an instrument used to observe or to measure the relationship between or among variables

valid: an instrument correctly measures the concepts being investigated or studied

uniform resource locators (URL): the address of each resource (file) on the Internet; it consists of the name of the computer system where the resource is stored, the directory path to the specific resource, and the file name

World Wide Web (WWW): an information service on the Internet based on a technology called hypertext

References

Butler, J. T. (1994). <u>Principles of health education and health promotion.</u> Englewood, CO: Morton.

Dignan, M. B., & Carr, P. A. (1992). <u>Program planning for health education and health promotion.</u> Philadelphia: Lea and Febiger.

Green, L. W., Kreuter, M. W., Deeds, S. G., & Patrick, K. B. (1980). <u>Health education planning: A diagnostic approach.</u> Palo Alto, CA: Mayfield.

National Task Force on the Preparation and Practice of Health Educators, Inc. (1985). <u>A framework for the development of competency-based curricula for entry-level health educators.</u> New York: Author.

Timmreck, T. C. (1995). <u>Planning, program development, and evaluation: A handbook for health promotion, aging, and health services.</u> Boston: Jones and Bartlett.

Windsor, R. A., Baranowski, T., Clark, N., & Cutter, G. (1984). <u>Evaluation of health promotion and education programs.</u> Palo Alto, CA: Mayfield.

Notes

2   *Planning Effective Health Education Programs*

Health education and health promotion are most often accomplished as programs (Dignan & Carr, 1992). According to the Joint Committee on Health Education Terminology [JCHET] (1991), a *health education program* is "a planned combination of activities developed with the involvement of specific populations and based on a needs assessment, sound principles of education, and periodic evaluation using a clear set of goals and objectives" (p. 179). The needs assessment preliminary step in program planning was described in Chapter 1. Two additional elements in the program planning process are implementation and evaluation. Implementation will be discussed in detail in Chapter 3 and evaluation in Chapter 4.

To develop a successful program, the health educator as planner must develop a set of *goals* and *objectives*. Objectives "clearly describe content and behavior, are appropriate for the particular target group, are stated in precise behavioral terms, and are measurable" (Dignan & Carr, 1992, p. 105). Educational *methods* and *learning activities* for achieving those goals and objectives are an integral part of the program plan as well (Dignan & Carr, 1992; Simons-Morton, Greene, & Gottlieb, 1995). A logical *scope* and *sequence* for the program must be developed for the target audience (Ames, Trucano, Wan, & Harris, 1995). In addition, *resources* as well as possible restrictions need to be identified (Dignan & Carr, 1992).

Community organizations, resource people, and program participants should be recruited and involved in the planning process and especially in the development of program objectives (Dignan & Carr, 1992, 1989; JCHET, 1991). Recruiting the actual planning group members is an integral part of the program planning process (Dignan & Carr, 1992). The following paragraphs describe aspects of program planning in the major health education settings.

Community Health Setting

In planning a violence prevention program, the health educator from the local health department seeks input and support from a variety of community agencies/organizations, individuals, and potential participants. The involvement of such people and organizations can enhance the program's success if their ideas and recommendations are considered during the program planning process.

Medical Setting

In planning a local hospital diabetes education program, the health educator determines what range of health information should be included. Needs assessment information identifies key areas to address, but the health educator then decides what specific knowledge, skills, and behaviors participants should acquire as a result of the program.

Post-Secondary Setting

In developing an acquaintance rape awareness program, the health educator, employed as a member of the university wellness program, targets men living in congregate housing (e.g., dormitories and fraternities). The health educator then chooses a variety of educational methods and learning activities to meet the program's objectives and to deliver the program content. Specific methods selected for the program are lecture, video, discussion, and role play.

School Setting

In planning for a comprehensive K-12 health education program, the school board decides to create a district-wide health *advisory board* to aid in portions of the planning process. The school board will seek 12-20 advisory board members and plans to solicit their input as to goals for the program through a *nominal group process.*

Worksite Setting

The XYZ Corporation wants to offer a smoking cessation program for its employees. The health educator employed by the corporation investigates the *resources* available within and beyond the community. For instance, the American Cancer Society may be contacted regarding the availability of a trained smoking cessation facilitator to conduct the sessions. In addition, the health educator needs to obtain company cooperation to provide employee incentives for participation. As part of effective planning, the health educator also identifies barriers to and constraints of the program that might hinder participation, then explores ways to reduce them if possible.

Planning Effective Health Education Programs

Competency A
Recruit community organizations, resource people, and potential participants for support and assistance in program planning.

Sub-Competency 1
Communicate need for the program to those whose cooperation will be essential.

Activity: Community Involvement: A Case Scenario

Student Outcome: The student can identify several methods of communicating the need for the program and specific strategies for getting key individual community members involved in the program planning process.

Directions:

1.   Consider the following case scenario:

         A needs assessment has identified an elderly assistance program as the top priority of a rural community of 7,000 people. Community organizations and resource people have been contacted and identified, but several of these people express little interest in becoming involved. All agree that it is a worthy and needed program, but few see how their input will be of benefit to the program or to themselves.

2.   List several methods of communicating the need for an elderly assistance program in your community.

3.   Identify strategies that might be used to convince key individuals in the community that they need to be involved in the planning process. Think about the types of priorities and motivations of various key agencies/organizations and how one can express the need for the elderly assistance program in ways that relate to their community jobs/roles.

Getting Started

The following text is a useful community organizing resource.

         Bracht, N. (Ed.). (1990). <u>Health promotion at the community level.</u> Newbury Park, CA: Sage.

Planning Effective Health Education Programs

Competency A
Recruit community organizations, resource people, and potential participants for support and assistance in program planning.

Sub-Competency 1
Communicate need for the program to those whose cooperation will be essential.

Activity: Recruitment Letter

Student Outcome: The student can express in written format the need for planning a specific health education program and solicit support and assistance to accomplish the planning task.

Directions:

1. Review proper format for writing a business letter before beginning this activity. English or business writing textbooks are good sources.

2. From data gathered in the activities on needs assessment, identify a program that is needed by a target population.

3. List all community organizations, resource people, and potential participants who may be able to provide support or assistance in planning the program.

4. Select one of those listed that is within the community you live, and using a real name and address, compose a letter which includes the following information:

    * Purpose or intent of letter
    * Your name, title, and organization
    * Target population for program planning
    * Area of emphasis of program
    * Justification of need for program
    * Solicitation of support from person to whom the letter is written
    * Means for person to respond to request

5. EXTRA CREDIT: Send the practice business letter to the actual person, but include a cover letter explaining the course assignment with a request to the individual to honestly critique your letter for its clarity, appropriateness of language, and ability to pique interest in supporting and assisting you in the hypothetical program planning process. Be sure to include a self-addressed, stamped envelope and a thank you for helping you in practicing skills for planning health education programs.

Getting Started

Brock, S. L. (1988). Better business writing (rev. ed.). Los Altos, CA: Crisp.

Planning Effective Health Education Programs

Competency A

Recruit community organizations, resource people, and potential participants for support and assistance in program planning.

Sub-Competency 2

Obtain commitment from personnel and decision makers who will be involved in the program.

Activity: Intent of Commitment

Student Outcome: The student can develop a form that identifies types of intent of commitment from others to assist in program planning.

Directions:

1. In small groups complete development of the partially developed "Intent of Commitment" form on the following page. Refinement of existing text or including additional information is encouraged.

2. List additional ways that community organizations, resource people, or volunteers may support and assist your efforts in program planning.

3. As a class combine various group ideas to finalize one form appropriate for use in the general community setting. Also, consider developing another form specific to a health education setting that requires different categories of support or assistance.

Intent of Commitment

Name and Title:

Organization:

Address:

Telephone/FAX:

Having been fully informed of the need for development of a health education program focusing on **(Name of Program of Topic Area)** and targeted to **(Identify Intended Audience)**, as a spokesperson for the above listed organization, I am indicating the following areas where support and assistance can be offered to **(Name of Sponsoring Agency/Organization)**.

_ _ _ _   Financial Assistance

_ _ _ _   Guest speakers

_ _ _ _   Publicity

_ _ _ _

_ _ _ _

_ _ _ _

_ _ _ _

_ _ _ _

_ _ _ _

_ _ _ _

_ _ _ _

_ _ _ _   Other (please explain in space provided below)

Signature _____   Date _____

Notes

Planning Effective Health Education Programs

Competency A
Recruit community organizations, resource people, and potential participants for support and assistance in program planning.

Sub-Competency 2
Obtain commitment from personnel and decision makers who will be involved in the program.

Activity: Operation Smoke Screen

Student Outcome: The student can identify and initiate contact with community members and agencies who will be involved in a community prevention/intervention program for smokers under age 18.

Directions:

1.   You have been asked to develop a community prevention and intervention program aimed at smokers under age 18.

2.   Identify at least 10 individuals and/or agencies within the community (by job title or agency type) whom you believe should be involved in the program.

3.   Compose a letter to be sent to these individuals or agencies which asks for their committed involvement in the program.

Planning Effective Health Education Programs

Competency A
Recruit community organizations, resource people, and potential participants for support and assistance in program planning.

Sub-Competency 3
Seek ideas and opinions of those who will affect or be affected by the program.

Activity: Recruiting And Utilizing An Advisory Board

Student Outcome: The student can identify appropriate individuals to include in goal setting via nominal group process.

Directions:

1.   Read the following case scenario, then respond to the questions below:

The local health department has received a federal violence prevention grant to be targeted at middle school aged youth in the community. The health department wishes to use an advisory board in the program planning process. The decision has been made to use the nominal group process with the advisory board to determine program goals. You have been asked to identify 12 people in the community to serve on the advisory board and then to facilitate the nominal group.

2.   Who would you invite to serve on the advisory board and why?

3.   Explain how you will conduct the goal setting activity using the nominal group process with the advisory board.

Getting Started

The following two references may be helpful in understanding the application of the nominal group process:

Fink, A., Kosecoff, J., Chassin, M., & Brook, R. H. (1984). Consensus methods: Characteristics and guidelines for use. American Journal of Public Health, 74, 979-983.

Van de Ven, A. H., & Delbecq, A. L. (1972). The nominal group as a research instrument for exploratory health studies. American Journal of Public Health, 62, 227-342.

Planning Effective Health Education Programs

Competency A
Recruit community organizations, resource people, and potential participants for support and assistance in program planning.

Sub-Competency 3
Seek ideas and opinions of those who will affect or be affected by the program.

Activity: Focus Group

Student Outcome: The student can plan a focus group for the purpose of seeking input for program direction.

Directions:

1.   Locate and review some of the resources about focus groups listed in "Getting Started."

2.   As a health educator in a university setting, you have been asked by the Student Life Advisory Committee to plan a women's wellness program. You decide to use focus groups to determine what issues are most important and should be addressed in the program. Organize your thoughts on the focus group by completing the information asked for in the Focus Group Worksheet on the following page.

Getting Started

Gilmore, G., & Campbell, M. (1996). Needs assessment strategies for health promotion and health education. Wisconsin: Brown and Benchmark.

Krueger, R. A. (1994). Focus groups: A practical guide for applied research (2nd ed.). Thousand Oaks, CA: Sage.

National Cancer Institute. (1992). Making health communication programs work: A planner's guide. (NIH Publication No. 92-1493/t068). Bethesda, MD: Author.

Wagnor, L. (1988). Focus groups when and how to use them: A practical guide. Palo Alto, CA: Stanford Center for Research in Disease Prevention, Health Promotion Resource Center.

Notes

FOCUS GROUP

Questions or Interview Guide
List below several questions you would ask that might provide insight for your program direction and focus.

Composition of Focus Group
Which individuals on campus might provide you with useful information about the issue or target group? List them below.

Recruiting
Describe how you will recruit focus group participants.

Incentives
What kind of incentives could you offer the participants for their time?

Setting
What location might be the best for your focus group?

Time Allocation
How long would your focus group session last?

Monitoring the Results
How will you record the participant responses?

Ground Rules
List any ground rules you would have for the participants during the focus group process.

Reporting
How will you report the results to the Advisory Committee?

Notes

Planning Effective Health Education Programs

Competency A
Recruit community organizations, resource people, and potential participants for support and assistance in program planning.

Sub-Competency 4
Incorporate feasible ideas and recommendations into the planning process.

Activity: Grouping, Judging, And Prioritizing What's Feasible

Student Outcome: The student can systematically prioritize worthy ideas and recommendations for planning a health education program.

Directions:

1.   Assume you have conducted a survey or focus group to gather feasible ideas and recommendations into the planning process of a new health education program for your agency/organization/institution.

2.   From the input you have received, there is a lengthy list of ideas and recommendations from others and now you need to determine what and how to use their ideas and suggestions.

3.   First, determine ways to group the ideas and recommendations by adding to the list below.

"Areas for Grouping Ideas and Recommendations"

1. Budget and Monetary Issues

2. Goals, Objectives, and Outcomes

3. Program Content

4. Publicity

5.

6.

7.

4. Second, identify criteria for determining the worth of the idea or recommendation as it applies <u>to each of the various areas</u> identified in step three of this activity. An example of possible criteria for Publicity is provided below. Practice adding additional criteria to this example before beginning on another area.

"Criteria for Judging Ideas and Recommendations"
Publicity Idea or Recommendation: <u>(Write in single idea here)</u>

Criterion 1   Monetary cost of implementation

           Feasible   Not feasible   Need more information

Criterion 2   Personnel needed for implementation

           Feasible   Not feasible   Need more information

Criterion 3

Criterion 4

Criterion 5

5. Last, determine a means for using the information gathered in step 4 of this activity to prioritize the ideas for each area. For example, will certain criteria have to be met before the idea has worth to be implemented? If so, which criteria must be considered? Or, can a point system be used to prioritize the ideas into those that have greater feasibility than others for program implementation? Describe your plan for prioritizing ideas and recommendations below.

"Plan for Prioritizing Ideas and Recommendations"

Planning Effective Health Education Programs

Competency B
Develop a logical scope and sequence plan for a health education program.

Sub-Competency 1
Determine the range of health information requisite to a given program of instruction.

<u>Activity: Cardio Plus Program</u>

Student Outcome: The student can delineate content areas and specific topics to be provided within a worksite cardiovascular risk reduction program.

Directions:

1.   Develop a cardiovascular risk reduction program, entitled the Cardio Plus Program, for employees at a mid-sized manufacturing company. The company's employees consist of males and females aged 19-62, employed in management and non-management positions. The employees have a wide range of cardiac health levels (heart healthy, diagnosis of early cardiovascular risk problems, and some who have been involved in cardiac rehabilitation programs). Management is very supportive of this program's development, implementation, and evaluation. The company also has an ongoing contract with a local health club. The program will be organized in six-week classes which meet at the worksite (or at the local health club) twice each week for one hour.

2.   The initial task is to identify at least six content areas for the program.

3.   Once the content areas have been chosen, delineate specific topics to be addressed within those content areas.

4.   Remember, the program consists of six weeks and 12 total one-hour sessions.

Planning Effective Health Education Programs

Competency B
Develop a logical scope and sequence plan for a health education program.

Sub-Competency 1
Determine the range of health information requisite to a given program of instruction.

<u>Activity: Reviewing The "Experts"</u>

Student Outcome: The student can demonstrate a valid method to determine the range of health information requisite to a given program of instruction.

Directions:

1.   If you are a school health education major, select a content area in health education that would be appropriate for high school age students. If you are a community health education major, select a topic area to be presented to a group of college students. Examples are a consumer health unit for high school students and environmental health for college students.

2.   Review at least two health textbooks, curricula, or teaching strategies resources appropriate for that age group. Your instructor may provide you with some materials or place some resources on reserve at the library.

3.   Make a list of the topics and subtopics listed in the table of contents for the selected content area.

4.   Assume you will have a total of four hours to cover this content area. From your listing of topics, select the ones you plan to include to teach.

5.   Write a one page paper justifying the topics and subtopics you chose.

<u>Getting Started</u>

Edlin, G., Golanty, Ed., & Brown, K. M. (1996). <u>Health and wellness</u> (5th ed.). Boston, MA: Jones and Bartlett.

Meeks, L., Heit, P., & Page, R. (1995). <u>Comprehensive school health education: Totally awesome strategies for teaching health</u> (2nd ed.). Blacklick, OH: Meeks and Heit.

Planning Effective Health Education Programs

Competency B
Develop a logical scope and sequence plan for a health education program.

Sub-Competency 2
Organize the subject areas comprising the scope of a program in logical sequence.

Activity: Cardio Plus Program II

Student Outcome: The student can logically and sequentially organize content areas and specific topics for a worksite cardiovascular risk reduction program.

Directions:

1.   Use the information recorded in the activity, "Cardio Plus Program" (p. 71). Organize the content areas and specific topics in a logical sequence.

2.   Decide which content areas will be addressed each week and the specific topics to be included in each one-hour session.

3.   Compare and discuss your sequence with others.

Getting Started

The following sources may be useful in understanding scope and sequence.

Ames, E. E., Trucano, L. A., Wan, J. C., & Harris, M. H. (1995). Designing school health curricula: Planning for good health (2nd ed.). Dubuque, IA: Brown and Benchmark.

Anspaugh, D. J., & Ezell, G. (1995). Teaching today's health (4th ed.). Boston: Allyn and Bacon.

Dignan, M. B., & Carr, P. A. (1992). Program planning for health education and promotion (2nd ed.). Philadelphia: Lea and Febiger.

Hoeger, W. W. K. (1987). The complete guide for the development and implementation of health promotion programs. Englewood, CO: Morton.

Planning Effective Health Education Programs

Competency B
Develop a logical scope and sequence plan for a health education program.

Sub-Competency 2
Organize the subject areas comprising the scope of a program in logical sequence.

Activity: **Place Your Order Please**

Student Outcome: The student can demonstrate the ability to justify a sequence of topics and subtopics for a selected subject area.

Directions:

1.   To prepare for this activity, review the list of topics selected for the activity, "Reviewing the Experts" (p. 72).

2.   Place the topics in a logical sequence; that is, what topic should be used to introduce the unit, what should follow next, and so on.

3.   Think carefully about what topics must be covered first before other topics can be understood.

4.   Develop a two-column overview of your sequence with justification as shown below. Continue numbering until your full sequence is listed. A sample format to use follows.

Content Area: **Target Group:**

Topic/Subtopic Area   Justification

_____

1.

2.

3.

4.

5.

Planning Effective Health Education Programs

Competency C
Formulate appropriate and measurable program objectives.

Sub-Competency 1
Infer educational objectives that facilitate achievement of specified competencies.

Activity: Developing Program Objectives

Student Outcome: The student can develop measurable objectives that are linked to a program goal.

Directions:

1.   Consider the following goal statement taken from Healthy People 2000: National Health Promotion and Disease Prevention Objectives:

> *To reduce the incidence of diabetic complications among older African Americans in the community.*

2.   Consider the following indicators relating to the achievement of the goal:

   a.   *Accurately assess blood sugar levels*
   b.   *Plan and follow a specific diet plan*
   c.   *Regulate blood pressure*
   d.   *Plan and follow a specific exercise program*

3.   Translate the indicators into measurable objectives using the following format:

EXAMPLE:
   Indicator A: Accurately assess blood sugar levels:

- **Eighty percent** of **the seniors in the program** will **accurately demonstrate the**
     criteria   target group   indicator/outcome
   proper use of a blood glucose machine   **to the health educator.**
                                                            condition.

· **By 5/20/96,**   **the participants in the program**   **will explain the blood test results**
     condition   target group   indicator/outcome
   with 100% accuracy.
         criteria

Getting Started

Cantor, J., Kaufman, N., & Klitzner, M. (1982). Four steps to better objectives. Madison: Wisconsin Clearinghouse.

Timmreck, T. C. (1995). Writing goals and objectives in planning, program development, and evaluation: A handbook for health promotion, aging, and health services. Boston: Jones and Bartlett.

DEVELOPING PROGRAM OBJECTIVES

Indicator B: Plan and follow a specific diet plan

By _____, _____, of _____
      condition   criteria/magnitude of change   target group

will _____
                             indicator/outcome

Indicator C: Regulate blood pressure

By _____, _____, of _____
      condition   criteria/magnitude of change   target group

will _____
                             indicator/outcome

Indicator D: Plan and follow a specific exercise program

By _____, _____, of _____
      condition   criteria/magnitude of change   target group

will _____
                             indicator/outcome

Notes

Planning Effective Health Education Programs

Competency C
Formulate appropriate and measurable program objectives.

Sub-Competency 1
Infer educational objectives that facilitate achievement of specified competencies.

Activity: Matching Objectives To Competencies

Student Outcome: The student can write an educational objective to facilitate achievement of a specific competency.

Directions:

1. For each of the following specified competencies write at least two specific instructional objectives.

2. Write the objectives underneath the specified competency. Each objective should include a verb that specifies a definite, observable participant behavior.

    a. The participant demonstrates the ability to plan heart healthy meals.

    b. The participant demonstrates effective communication skills in resolving conflicts.

    c. The participant demonstrates the ability to access reliable, valid health information from a variety of sources.

    d. The participant demonstrates the ability to choose appropriate times for self medication and when to seek professional help.

Planning Effective Health Education Programs

Competency C
Formulate appropriate and measurable program objectives.

Sub-Competency 2
Develop a framework of broadly stated, operational objectives relevant to a proposed health education program.

Activity: Broad Program Objectives

Student Outcome: The student can develop broad or general instructional objectives for a specified health education program.

Directions:

1.   Choose one of the four following proposed health education programs:

   a. An abstinence based sex education program for two weeks at a junior high school. Co-ed class meets 45 minutes daily.

   b. A nutrition program for single and married senior citizens with one and one-half hour sessions per month with a total length of two months.

   c. A five session, one hour per session, cancer awareness and prevention program for women of any given community. The final session is to be scheduled by the participant for a free mammogram.

   d. A three hour sun protection program offered to day care directors, their employees, and parents of the children.

2.   First, give a name to the program and next write appropriate educational goals for the chosen program.

3.   To demonstrate your understanding of the difference between a broad educational objective, often called a goal, and a specific instructional objective, write one specific instructional objective for one of the educational objectives.

Getting Started

   Gilbert, G. G., & Sawyer, R. G. (1995). Health education: Creating strategies for school and community health. Boston: Jones and Bartlett.

Planning Effective Health Education Programs

Competency C
Formulate appropriate and measurable program objectives.

Sub-Competency 2
Develop a framework of broadly stated, operational objectives relevant to a proposed health education program.

Activity: Levels Of Program Objectives

Student Outcome: The student can develop a hierarchy of program objectives.

Directions:

1.   Select a health issue and target group. (It may be easiest to choose a statement from Healthy People 2000: National Health Promotion and Disease Prevention Objectives that would already identify an issue and target group.)

2.   Develop an objective for each of the following levels listed in the hierarchy below. Refer to the sample objectives on the following page.

Levels of Program Objectives
Awareness
Knowledge
Attitudes
Skill Development
Access
Behavior
Risk Reduction
Health Status

Getting Started

McKenzie, J. F., & Smeltzer, J. L. (1997). Planning, implementing, and evaluating health promotion programs: A primer (2nd ed.). Boston: Allyn and Bacon.

Parkinson, R. S., & Associates. (1982). Managing health promotion in the workplace: Guidelines for implementing and evaluation. Palo Alto, CA: Mayfield.

U.S. Department of Health & Human Services. (1991). Healthy people 2000: National health promotion and disease prevention objectives for the nation. (Public Health Service Publication No. 91-50212). Washington, DC: Government Printing Office.

LEVELS OF PROGRAM OBJECTIVES (SAMPLE)

Goal: To reduce the incidence of diabetic complications among older African Americans.

Awareness Objective:
After completing a health risk survey at the end of the first session, at least 80% of the participants will be able to identify their personal risk factors for developing health problems associated with their diabetes.

Knowledge Objective:
After listening to a lecture on Diabetic Complications, participants in the program will list three out of five of the most common health problems experienced by diabetics.

Attitude Objective:
After participating in small group discussions, participants will score at least 4.0 or above on a Likert scale inventory assessing their acceptance of the implications of having diabetes.

Skill Development Objective:
By the second week of the program, participants will demonstrate how to use a home glucose meter by "reading" the blood sugar levels with 100% accuracy each time in a practice session.

Access Objective:
By the third week of the program, all participants will be given the opportunity to have an eye examination to screen for diabetic retinopathy.

Behavior Objective:
Three months after the program is completed, at least 50% of the participants will be involved in daily exercise programs as assessed by a follow-up questionnaire.

Risk Reduction Objective:
Six months after the program, participants surveyed will reveal that they have reduced or eliminated at least one risk factor identified in their original health risk survey taken at the beginning of the program.

Health Status Objective:
One year after the program, the hospital admission rate for diabetic complications among the participants will be 50% lower than those diabetics who did not attend the program.

LEVELS OF PROGRAM OBJECTIVES

Goal:

Awareness Objective:

Knowledge Objective:

Attitude Objective:

Skill Development Objective:

Access Objective:

Behavior Objective:

Risk Reduction Objective:

Health Status Objective:

Notes

Planning Effective Health Education Programs

Competency D
Design educational programs consistent with specified program objectives.

Sub-Competency 1
Match proposed learning activities with those implicit in the stated objectives.

Activity: A Perfect Match

Student Outcome: The student can correlate learning objectives with appropriate learning activities.

Directions:

1.   Access any health-related book in which health activities, strategies, or methods are described to enhance learning. Identify two of the activities.

2.   Review objectives as identified in either Healthy People 2000 or The National Health Education Standards. In the latter source, objectives are labeled as "Performance Indicators."

3.   Match the activity to an appropriate objective identified in these documents.

4.   Write a paragraph explaining why the learning activity and objective are correlated appropriately. Do this for both activities selected.

Getting Started

Joint Committee on National Education Standards. (1995). National health education standards. Atlanta, GA: American Cancer Society.

U. S. Department of Health & Human Services. (1992). Healthy people 2000: National health promotion and disease prevention objectives. Washington, DC: Government Printing Office.

Planning Effective Health Education Programs

Competency D
Design educational programs consistent with specified program objectives.

Sub-Competency 1
Match proposed learning activities with those implicit in the stated objectives.

<u>Activity:</u> <u>Selecting Appropriate Learning Activities To Meet Objectives</u>

Student Outcome: The student can create learning activities to meet stated objectives.

Directions:

1.   Refer to the objectives developed in the activity, "Broad Program Objectives" (p. 80). For at least two objectives, plan two learning activities. The two learning activities for each objective should target audiences in different settings.

2.   Provide an outline describing each learning activity in sufficient detail so that someone not familiar with it could conduct it.

3.   List and discuss several factors that influence the selection of learning activities.

<u>Getting Started</u>

Talk with a health educator in any of the five major settings and ask about the types of learning activities they utilize most often and in what situations.

Ames, E. A., Trucano, L. A., Wan, J. C., & Harris, M. H. (1995). <u>Designing school health curricula</u> (2nd ed.). Dubuque, IA: Brown and Benchmark.

Gilbert, G. G., & Sawyer, R. (1995). <u>Health education: Creating strategies for school and community health.</u> Boston: Jones and Bartlett.

Greenberg, J. S. (1995). <u>Health education: Learner-centered instructional strategies</u> (3rd ed.). Dubuque, IA: Wm. C. Brown.

Meeks, L. B., & Heit, P. (1996). <u>Comprehensive school education.</u> Blacklick, OH: Meeks and Heit.

Planning Effective Health Education Programs

Competency D
Design educational programs consistent with specified program objectives.

Sub-Competency 2
Formulate a wide variety of alternative educational methods.

Activity: Educational Methods For The Senses

Student Outcome: The student can develop a wide variety of alternative educational methods utilized for health programs.

Directions:

1.   Brainstorm a list of educational methods designed to present educational material. Gilbert and Sawyer's (1995) book is an excellent source of information regarding instructional methods and describes numerous methods in detail.

2.   Consider all the senses (i.e., sight, sound, touch, taste, and smell) when developing this list. Indicate which methods involve the various senses or combination of senses.

3.   Choose 5-10 methods and identify several advantages and disadvantages of each (e.g., the use of anatomical models can provide for extensive variety and "hands-on" experience, but can also be expensive and require extra setup).

Getting Started

The following provide sources of information regarding educational methods:

Fodor, J. T., Dalis, G. T., & Giarrantano, S. C. (1995). Health instruction: Theory and application (5th ed.). Baltimore, MD: Williams and Wilkins.

Gilbert, G. G., & Sawyer, R. G. (1995). Health education: Creating strategies for school and community health. Boston: Jones and Bartlett.

Greenberg, J. S. (1995). Health education learner-centered instructional strategies (3rd ed.). Dubuque, IA: Brown and Benchmark.

Ramirez, S. (1994). Health promotion for all: Strategies for reaching diverse populations at the workplace. Omaha, NE: Wellness Councils of America.

Notes

Planning Effective Health Education Programs

Competency D
Design educational programs consistent with specified program objectives.

Sub-Competency 2
Formulate a wide variety of alternative educational methods.

Activity: Educational Strategies Resource File

Student Outcome: The student can identify and list strengths and weaknesses of a wide variety of educational strategies.

Directions:

1.   Research the following teaching strategies:

brainstorming	field trips	problem solving/decision-making
buzz groups	guest speakers	role play
cartoons	lecture	self-appraisal
cooperative learning	lecture/discussion	simulation
debate	mass media	student presentations
demonstrations	models	values clarification
displays/bulletin boards	panel discussion	peer education

2.   Using one index card per strategy, record the following information (see sample on the next page):

* brief description of the strategy
* strengths of the strategy
* weaknesses of the strategy
* suggestions for use (e.g., age group, content area, learning style)

Getting Started

The following books are excellent resources for this activity. If they are not available in your library or through interlibrary loan, check with faculty members to see if they might have a copy they are willing to lend out.

Ames, E. A., Trucano, L. A., Wan, J. C., & Harris, M. H. (1995). Designing school health curricula (2nd ed.). Dubuque, IA: Brown and Benchmark.

Gilbert, G. G., & Sawyer, R. (1995). Health education: Creating strategies for school and community health. Boston: Jones and Bartlett.

Greenberg, J. S. (1995). Health education: Learner-centered instructional strategies (3rd ed.). Dubuque, IA: Wm. C. Brown.

Meeks, L. B., & Heit, P. (1992). Comprehensive school health: Totally awesome teaching strategies. Blacklick, OH: Meeks and Heit.

EDUCATIONAL STRATEGIES RESOURCE FILE

Front

Education Strategy/Method:

Description:

Strengths	Weaknesses

1.   1.

2.   2.

3.   3.

(e.g., age group, content areas, etc.)

Back

Suggestions for Use (e.g., age group, content area, etc.):

Notes

Planning Effective Health Education Programs

Competency D
Design educational programs consistent with specified program objectives.

Sub-Competency 3
Select strategies best suited to implementation of educational objectives
in a given setting.

Activity: Instructional Strategies Exploration

Student Outcome: The student can delineate strategies best suited to the implementation of drug education, human sexuality, cardiovascular health, consumer health, nutrition, and first aid/CPR programs to diverse populations.

Directions:

1.   Individuals from four community groups have asked that you provide 60-90 minute programs addressing each of the following content areas: Drug Education, Human Sexuality, Cardiovascular Health, Consumer Health, Nutrition, and First Aid/CPR.

2.   The population groups include: inner city junior high students, parochial high school students, young adults (aged 18-24) employed in a local factory, and participants from a local senior citizen center.

3.   Using the information gathered in the activity, "Educational Methods for the Senses" (p. 87), indicate on the worksheet which methods are appropriate for each population and content area.

4.   Compare and justify your choices with others.

Getting Started

Fodor, J. T., Dalis, G. T., & Giarrantano, S. C. (1995). Health instruction: Theory and application (5th ed.). Baltimore, MD: Williams and Wilkins.

Gilbert, G. G., & Sawyer, R. G. (1995). Health education: Creating strategies for school and community health. Boston: Jones and Bartlett.

Ramirez, S. (1994). Health promotion for all: Strategies for reaching diverse populations at the workplace. Omaha, NE: Wellness Councils of America.

Notes

INSTRUCTIONAL STRATEGIES EXPLORATION

Directions: Using the information gathered in "Educational Methods for the Senses," indicate (with a ✔) the instructional methods appropriate for inner city junior high students (jh), parochial high school students (hs), young adults (aged 18-24) employed in a local factory (ya), and participants from a local senior citizen center (ad) for each of the content areas.

INSTRUCTIONAL METHOD	DRUG EDUCATION				HUMAN SEXUALITY				CARDIO HEALTH				CONSUMER HEALTH				NUTRITION				FIRST AID/ CPR			
	jh	hs	ya	ad	jh	hs	ya	ad	jh	hs	ya	ad	jh	hs	ya	ad	jh	hs	ya	ad	jh	hs	ya	ad

Notes

Planning Effective Health Education Programs

Competency D
Design educational programs consistent with specified program objectives.

Sub-Competency 3
Select strategies best suited to implementation of educational objectives
in a given setting.

Activity: Selecting The Best Strategy

Student Outcome: The student can demonstrate justification for selection of a strategy for a given educational objective.

Directions:

1.   Refer to list of topics by scope and sequence in the activity, "Place Your Order, Please" (p. 74).

2.   Develop three *cognitive* and three *affective* objectives for your educational program.

3.   Under each objective, list one or two teaching strategies (brainstorming, guest speaker, for example) that you would utilize to help in achieving that objective.

4.   Under each strategy, provide a short justification. For example:

Cognitive Objective:

   Strategy Selected:

      Justification:

         Student Outcome: The student...

Planning Effective Health Education Programs

Competency D
Design educational programs consistent with specified program objectives.

Sub-Competency 4
Plan a sequence of learning opportunities building upon and reinforcing mastery
of preceding objectives.

<u>Activity: Health Education Scope And Sequence</u>

Student Outcome: The student can arrange objectives and learning activities in logical, age-appropriate sequence.

Directions:

1.   Consider the following objective taken from <u>Healthy People 2000: National Health Promotion and Disease Prevention Objectives</u> dealing with tobacco use and youth:

   Reduce the initiation of cigarette smoking by children and youth so that
   no more than 15% have become regular cigarette smokers by age 20.

2.   Review information on the "scope and sequence" of health education content found in the resources listed in "Getting Started."

3.   Arrange the objectives listed below in a logical "sequence" for inclusion in a comprehensive health education program. Mark each objective with 1, 5, or 8, or 12 to show at which grade level the objective should be addressed:

   1 = first grade   5 = fifth grade   8 = eighth grade   12 = twelfth grade

   > **EXAMPLE:**
   > _8_ Can analyze advertisements for tobacco products

   ___Can compare and contrast various smoking cessation methods
   ___Can identify nicotine as a "drug"
   ___Recognizes a "peer pressure" situation
   ___Identifies peer and adult influences on smoking choices
   ___Can list alternatives to drug use

4.   Suggest at least one learning activity for the four different objectives listed below (see example).

   ___Can describe how tobacco was used many years ago
   ___Can discuss the harmful effects of smoking during pregnancy
   ___Can identify the dangers associated with smoking clove cigarettes
   ___Can identify reasons why people choose not to smoke

HEALTH EDUCATION SCOPE AND SEQUENCE

EXAMPLE:
Objective: Analyze advertisements for tobacco products (Grade 8)
Activity: Students will collect tobacco advertisements from magazines. In small groups, the students will organize their ads by "themes." Groups will share their results.

Objective:

Activity:

Objective:

Activity:

Objective:

Activity:

Objective:

Activity:

<u>Getting Started</u>

Any state frameworks for health education or a teacher's edition of grade-specific health textbooks can be used.

Bruess, C., & Gay, J. (1987). <u>Implementing comprehensive school health.</u> New York: Macmillan.

Creswell, W., & Newman, I. (1989). <u>School health practice.</u> St. Louis, MO: Times Mirror/Mosby.

School Health Education Study. (1967). <u>Health education: A conceptual approach to curriculum design.</u> St. Paul, MN: 3M Education Press.

Planning Effective Health Education Programs

Competency D
Design educational programs consistent with specified program objectives.

Sub-Competency 4
Plan a sequence of learning opportunities building upon and reinforcing mastery of preceding objectives.

Activity: Strategy Sequence Discussion

Student Outcome: The student can order a number of learning opportunities into a meaningful sequence.

Directions:

1.   Divide class into groups of three students.

2.   Select a Healthy People 2000 objective that is of interest to you. Decide whether the objective pertains to a school-based or community-based approach. Make sure each group has selected a different objective.

3.   Write the objective at the top of the page. In your group, brainstorm at least four learning activities that you believe would be appropriate to help meet the objective.

4.   Discuss in your group the sequence of activities. What should come first and why? What is next and why, and so on?

5.   Each group should report the results of the discussion by writing the objective on the board followed by the four learning activities. One member of the group will explain the justification for the sequence of activities.

Getting Started

Gilbert, G. G., & Sawyer, R. G. (1995). Health education: Creating strategies for school and community health. Boston: Jones and Bartlett.

U. S. Department of Health & Human Services. (1992). Healthy People 2000: National Health Promotion and Disease Prevention Objectives. Washington, DC: Government Printing Office.

Notes

Glossary of Terms

advisory board: a group formed to provide advice on a variety of topics and to serve as advocates; members of the group are selected from broad-based segments of the community, including but not limited to parents, students, city officials, community health agencies, clergy, health professionals, and others

affective: the domain of learning which refers to the examination of feelings, attitudes, and emotions

cognitive: the domain of learning which refers to the acquisition and application of knowledge

health education program: a planned combination of activities developed with the involvement of specific populations and based on a needs assessment, sound principles of education, and periodic evaluation using a clear set of goals and objectives

goals: broad statements of direction used to present the overall intent of a program or course; they do not need to be stated in measurable terms

learning activities: application of teaching methods to specific learning objectives

objectives: the intended outcomes of instruction; should be stated in measurable terms

methods: techniques used by an educator for the purpose of accomplishing the educational objectives

nominal group process: a structured meeting that involves an orderly procedure for obtaining information from target population groups who are closely associated with a specific problem

resources: sources of information or help that can be used to enhance learning

scope: the range of health topics to be included in a curriculum or program

sequence: the order or arrangement of topics/subject matter in a curriculum or program

Notes

References

Ames, E. A., Trucano, L. A., Wan, J. C., & Harris, M. H. (1995). Designing school health curricula (2nd ed.). Dubuque, IA: Brown and Benchmark.

Bracht, N. (1990). Health promotion at the community level. Newbury Park, CA: Sage.

Dignan, M. B., & Carr, P. A. (1992). Program planning for health education and promotion. Philadelphia: Lea and Febiger.

Joint Committee on Health Education Terminology. (1991). Report of the 1990 joint committee on health education terminology. Journal of Health Education, 22 (3), 173-184.

Simons-Morton, B. G., Greene, W. H., & Gottlieb, N. H. (1995). Introduction to health education and health promotion (2nd ed.). Prospect Heights, IL: Waveland.

Notes

3   *Implementing Health Education Programs*

The third step in health education program development requires the design of a process that will allow the health educator to put the written plan into action. In Chapter 1, the needs assessment process which helped identify a target group and the specific health needs of the target population was addressed. In Chapter 2, the focus was on planning for the health education program through the development of appropriate goals, objectives, and strategies. This chapter addresses *implementation*, the process of setting up, managing, and executing a project (Timmreck, 1995). Specifically, implementation involves the initiation and development of a set of recommendations to guide the planner in using methods, techniques, materials, and resources to accomplish what has been planned (National Task Force on Preparation and Practice of Health Educators, 1985; Parkinson, 1982; Ross & Mico, 1980; Timmreck, 1995).

The health educator must be capable of executing or delivering planned educational programs. To do so, the planner must become familiar with educational methods, techniques, and instructional media that will provide the best and most appropriate learning situations for individuals in the identified target group (McKenzie & Smeltzer, 1997). This includes such things as exploring the advantages and disadvantages of *experiential* activities, categorizing methods as individual or group-centered, identifying the strengths and weaknesses of specific types of instructional media, and comparing the effectiveness of alternative methods in reaching specific objectives (National Task Force on Preparation and Practice of Health Educators, 1985).

In order to meet the objectives stated for the program, the target group should have certain skills or knowledge that will enable them to take action. *Enabling factors* include skills and resources of the target group or attributes of the health care delivery system that have the potential to influence health (Dignan & Carr, 1992; Green & Krueter, 1991). To assess the target group's potential for successfully achieving the program objectives, the planner will need to pretest the abilities and knowledge of the participants. From the results of the pretest data, enabling objectives can be designed as needed to bring all of the learners to a common starting point before fully implementing the program. For example, a pretest given to the participants as part of their registration process could identify terminology deficiencies that should be addressed early in the planned program.

Methods and media should be carefully selected to properly match the characteristics of the learner. The planner will need to identify criteria for creating a system to evaluate and select appropriate methods (Ames, Trucano, Wan, & Harris, 1995). Criteria for program methods and media selection include learner characteristics, such as cultural background, socioeconomic status, and educational level. In addition, participants will need to be analyzed to determine learning styles (McKenzie & Smeltzer, 1997). Although a method may be an appropriate match to learner needs and characteristics, other criteria for final selection should be considered. Resources needed for incorporation of a specific method vary according to factors of time, personnel, money, and equipment. Ultimately selected methods must be both effective for the learner and program objectives, yet efficient in terms of available resources. Appropriateness of method to achieving the intended objectives is yet another key criteria for method selection.

Monitoring the program during its implementation will be necessary to facilitate adjustments in objectives and activities. During program implementation some type of formal process evaluation, such as planned participant feedback, or informal evaluation, such as daily observations, will provide direction for needed change. Based on the findings, immediate decisions may be made, preferably by collaboration of planner and participants, to revise, add, or eliminate planned methods, activities, or objectives. Components of the program such as time lines, budget, personnel, and number of participants being served also should be monitored to determine if the program is successfully meeting its implementation goals.

Putting the program successfully into action is a vital component which follows program planning. The implementation phase requires detailed planning and specified guidelines on the part of the health educator. The next few paragraphs will provide specific examples of the implementation process occurring in a variety of health education settings.

Community Health Setting

A prevention program aimed at reducing the incidence of complications among diabetics in the community was developed and is currently being implemented. The health educator, as part of the planning process, devised a system for monitoring the program to assess the relevance of existing program objectives to current needs. After each session, the health educator asks the participants to complete a questionnaire concerning the material that was covered in the session and what their expectations are for the next meeting. Based upon the results, the health educator makes revisions in program activities and objectives as necessary as the program is being implemented.

Medical Setting

The health educators in a hospital are contemplating the development of a series of educational videos that would be available to patients in their rooms through the hospital TV channel. In a planning session, a series of questions and issues are identified concerning the implementation of such a program. First, the health educators want to know the success of the media in promoting achievement of educational programs such as the one being considered. Secondly, the health educators determine that an inventory of personnel, time, and equipment is necessary to identify barriers and constraints to implementing the program. Thirdly, the health educators decide to evaluate whether existing videos are appropriate. If new videos are to be produced, the planners desire to know costs involved.

Post-Secondary Setting

A "Self Care" program is being offered to all students by the Wellness Center at a university. The health educator decides to employ a variety of educational methods and techniques in implementing the program. Based on a review of the literature concerning the learning styles of the target population, the health educator selects educational strategies experiential in nature and group-centered over individual-centered strategies.

School Setting

The health educator at the local middle school is in charge of developing a smoking prevention curriculum for the eighth graders. Since the school has a culturally diverse population, the methods and material to be selected need to be sensitive to the cultural differences of the participants. To facilitate this process, the health educator arranges for a pilot group of students from the ninth grade class to review the materials. The health educator develops a checklist to assist the pilot group in evaluating the materials for culturally insensitive language and actions.

Worksite Setting

A first aid and safety program is being implemented by a county health department educator for the employees at a local business. During the first session, the health educator asks participants to complete both a written and skills pretest to determine the current relationship of their knowledge to the proposed program objectives. After reviewing the results, the health educator decides to omit the basic first aid information and move directly to

the advanced first aid skills and knowledge.

Implementing Health Education Programs

Competency A
Exhibit competence in carrying out planned programs.

Sub-Competency 1
Employ a wide range of educational methods and techniques.

<u>Activity: Activities Sequence</u>

Student Outcome: The student can develop a sequence of educational methods/techniques which progress from simple to complex.

Directions:

1.   Pair five specific populations with five content areas. For example:

        * WIC participants and nutrition
        * High school students and sexuality education
        * Factory employees and safety issues

2.   Using information gathered in the activity, "Educational Strategies Resource File" (p. 89), develop a sequence of educational methods/techniques for each of the pairings which progresses from simple to complex. For example, a sequence of nutrition activities for WIC participants may begin with brainstorming a list of quick and easy to prepare dinner foods, progress to a group discussion regarding the nutritional merit of each item, and culminate in a demonstration of the preparation of a nutritionally sound dinner.

3.   Compare and justify your choices with others.

Implementing Health Education Programs

Competency A
Exhibit competence in carrying out planned programs.

Sub-Competency 1
Employ a wide range of educational methods and techniques.

Activity: Volunteer Program Presentation

Student Outcome: The student can demonstrate the use of several educational methods and techniques during a presentation.

Directions:

1.   Volunteer to deliver a health related presentation or program either as an individual or with a small group.

2.   Use three or more educational methods or techniques in the presentation. It is essential that methods and techniques be selected that will achieve the intended objectives.

3.   Write a short paper reflecting on your abilities to use several educational methods. Discuss your comfort level with different methods and ways to improve your use of them.

Getting Started

Contact any local organization that schedules health related presentations or programs and volunteer to present a program. Some possible organizations to contact include: local chapter of Eta Sigma Gamma, any health related volunteer organizations on campus, the university wellness center, any area voluntary health agency (e.g., American Cancer Society), and the local health department.

Implementing Health Education Programs

Competency A
Exhibit competence in carrying out planned programs.

Sub-Competency 2
Apply individual or group process methods as appropriate to given learning situations.

Activity: HIV Cooperative Learning Activity

Student Outcome: The student can plan and implement a cooperative learning activity using recommended procedures for effective implementation.

Directions:

1.   Develop a learning activity on HIV infection for a target audience of teenagers using one of the following cooperative learning strategies: corners, pairs check, roundrobin, roundtable, think-pair-share, or team word webbing.

2.   Complete the first five steps on the following page as the planning phase.

3.   Conduct the activity during a class or volunteer to deliver the planned cooperative learning activity to a chosen audience, if possible.

4.   During and immediately following the activity, follow steps 6-9 as identified on the chart on the following page.

Getting Started

For explanations of the various cooperative learning strategies, see:

Cinelli, B., Symons, C. W., Bechtel, L., & Rose-Colley, M. (1994). Applying cooperative learning in health education practice. Journal of School Health, 64 (3), 99-102.

Kagan, S. (1990). The structural approach to cooperative learning. Educational Leadership, 47 (4), 12-15.

HIV COOPERATIVE LEARNING ACTIVITY*

1.   **Academic and Group Objectives**

2.   **Group Size/Method for Assigning Participants to Groups**

3.   **Room Arrangement (diagram)**

4.   **Student Roles and Job Descriptions (e.g., Recorder, Reporter, Manager, etc.)**

5.   **Task, Criteria for Success, and Desired Behaviors During Group Activity (instructions)**

6.   **Monitor Student Behavior and Interactions**
7.   **Act as a Consultant and Facilitator to the Groups**
8.   **Intervene, as Needed, to Teach Social Skills**

9.   **Evaluate Student Learning, Use of Stated Skills, Group Functioning; Offer Feedback on Group Achievement**

* Steps taken from Johnson, D. W., Johnson, R. T., & Smith K. (1991). Active learning in the college classroom. Edina, MN: Interaction Book Company.

Notes

Implementing Health Education Programs

Competency A
Exhibit competence in carrying out planned programs.

Sub-Competency 2
Apply individual or group process methods as appropriate to given learning situations.

Activity: Is "Experience" The Best Teacher?

Student Outcome: The student can define experiential learning, identify appropriate teaching methods, and analyze the best use of those methods in different situations.

Directions:

1.   To successfully complete this activity, first locate two sources that define "experiential learning" or "experiential activities." Using the following worksheet, complete steps one through five. Record those definitions and also reference the sources.

2.   Next list and define two teaching methods that provide experiential learning. List and define two methods that are not experiential.

3.   List the advantages of developing a lesson plan or presentation using methods that involve experiential learning.

4.   Are there situations in which more passive teaching methods would be better than experiential learning? If so, identify one.

5.   To finish this activity, complete the open-ended statements listed on the worksheet.

Notes

IS "EXPERIENCE" THE BEST TEACHER?

1.   List at least two definitions of "experiential learning." Make sure the references are included.

2a.   <u>Identify</u> and <u>define</u> two teaching methods that include experiential learning.

b.   <u>Identify</u> and <u>define</u> two teaching methods that are not experiential.

3.   What are two advantages of utilizing experiential teaching methods in developing lesson plans for school or community settings?

4.   Identify one situation in which a more passive teaching method might be better than experiential learning.

5.   I learn best when the instructor . . .

      I prefer to learn by . . .

      I find it difficult to learn when . . .

Notes

Implementing Health Education Programs

Competency A
Exhibit competence in carrying out planned programs.

Sub-Competency 3
Utilize instructional equipment and other instructional media.

Activity: Instructional Equipment And Media Exploration

Student Outcome: The student can describe how to operate selected instructional equipment and select appropriate instructional media for use with each piece of equipment.

Directions:

1. Develop a checklist of steps involved in operating five of the following pieces of audiovisual equipment: audiotape recorder, film projector (usually 16 mm), filmstrip projector, freestanding projector screen, opaque projector, overhead projector, slide projector, television, video camcorder, and VCR.

2. Identify types of instructional media and describe how each type can be effectively selected and evaluated for use with the above equipment.

3. Identify the strengths and weaknesses of various types of instructional media/equipment pertinent to specific ages, group sizes, and populations.

Getting Started

The following source provides excellent information about instructional equipment and media:

Gilbert, G. G., & Sawyer, R. G. (1995). Health education: Creating strategies for school and community health. Boston: Jones and Bartlett.

Implementing Health Education Programs

Competency A
Exhibit competence in carrying out planned programs.

Sub-Competency 3
Utilize instructional equipment and other instructional media.

Activity: Media Check-Off

Student Outcome: The student can demonstrate competence in the use of a variety of instructional media and equipment.

Directions:

1.   Schedule an appointment with the appropriate center/unit (e.g., Instructional Media Center) to receive training on any equipment or type of media with which you are not familiar or competent in using.

2.   If such a service exists on a community college or university campus, schedule an appointment to be tested on a variety of equipment/media. Be sure to ask about location of extra bulbs and procedures for replacing blown bulbs in equipment.

3.   Talk to several practicing health educators about their use of media equipment. What do they use most often? Why? Practical hints for media use?

Getting Started

Chapter 5 of the following text offers a useful description/discussion of a variety of instructional media and equipment:

Gilbert, G. G., & Sawyer, R. G. (1995). Health education: Creating strategies for school and community health. Boston: Jones and Bartlett.

Implementing Health Education Programs

Competency A
Exhibit competence in carrying out planned programs.

Sub-Competency 4
Select methods that best facilitate practice of program objectives.

Activity: Violence Prevention Program

Student Outcome: The student can choose appropriate methods and activities for accomplishing stated program objectives.

Directions:

1.   Use the "Violence Prevention Program" chart on the following page.

2.   For each objective, identify several appropriate methods to use in accomplishing the objective. List a minimum of two methods in the space provided to the right of each objective.

3.   Be prepared to defend the methods listed on the chart.

Getting Started

It may be helpful to talk with elementary school teachers for input regarding appropriate methods to use with lower elementary grade level children.

Notes

VIOLENCE PREVENTION PROGRAM

Objectives	Methods									
1. Increase teacher knowledge, skill, and application regarding use of a violence prevention curriculum.										
2. Increase student knowledge of pro-social skills (i.e., please, thank you, asking permission, etc.)										
3. Increase student application of pro-social skills.										
4. Increase student knowledge of decision-making and problem-solving skills.										
5. Increase student application of decision-making and problem-solving skills.										
6. Increase parental knowledge of violence prevention education.										
7. Increase parental application of violence prevention skills.										
8. Increase student opportunities to utilize and apply violence prevention skills.										
9. Increase student opportunities to be recognized for utilizing and applying violence prevention skills.										

Source: Form 0630-95 Prevention Work Plan, Illinois Department of Alcohol & Substance Abuse, Chicago, IL, 1995. Used by permission.

Notes

Implementing Health Education Programs

Competency A
Exhibit competence in carrying out planned programs.

Sub-Competency 4
Select methods that best facilitate practice of program objectives.

Activity: Match Maker

Student Outcome: The student can select appropriate instructional methods to be used in achieving program objectives.

Directions:

1.   Review objectives delineated in Healthy People 2000. Choose five objectives.

2.   Using the list generated in the activity, "Educational Methods For The Senses" (p. 87), match an instructional method with an objective.

3.   Describe the potential effectiveness of each method in achieving the objectives.

Getting Started

The following source provides excellent information about instructional methods:

Gilbert, G. G., & Sawyer, R. G. (1995). Health education: Creating strategies for school and community health. Boston: Jones and Bartlett.

Implementing Health Education Programs

Competency B
Infer enabling objectives as needed to implement instructional programs
in specified settings.

Sub-Competency 1
Pretest learners to ascertain present abilities and knowledge relative to proposed
program objectives.

Activity: Ranking And Revising

Student Outcome: The student can develop a pretest in order to ascertain knowledge level of
learners prior to program implementation.

Directions:

1.   Although there are several types of questions that can be developed to measure levels
        of knowledge, one method would be to have program participants or students respond
        to a rank order activity.

2.   Locate a general health education textbook (sometimes referred to as a personal health
        text). Select a health topic that might be the subject of a one-week unit in school or a
        seminar in community health. For example, select "Cardiovascular Disease" or
        "HIV/AIDS."

3.   Using the material in the textbook, make a list of the subtopics that you would include
        in your lesson or program (see "Getting Started" for example).

4.   Develop a one page handout listing all of the subtopics. Also include a set of
        directions to the learner asking him/her to rank order the list of subtopics. For
        example, if there are 10 subtopics, a rank of 1 would be placed next to the subtopic in
        which the learner felt <u>most</u> knowledgeable. The remaining 9 subtopics would then be
        ranked, with number 10 referring to the subtopic in which the learner felt <u>least</u>
        knowledgeable.

5.   In groups of 6-8 students, hand out the ranking sheets and have individuals rank order
        the subtopics. Each group member should administer his/her ranking sheet to others in
        the small group.

6.   Tally responses to the ranking sheet. Based upon the data, write a one page
        summary paper addressing the following questions:

        a.   What does the data indicate about participants' knowledge of subtopics?

b.   Are the results different in any way from what you expected? Explain why or
        why not.

c.   Describe the importance of pretesting learners. How might it influence the
        program implementation?

7.   Hand in a copy of the ranking sheet, data analysis sheet, and one page summary to the
        instructor.

Getting Started

Content Area: HIV/AIDS

_____ Differences between HIV and AIDS
_____ Drug Therapies
_____ Immune System
_____ Opportunistic Infections
_____ Prevention Strategies
_____ Statistical Overview
_____ Understanding the Virus
_____ Universal Precautions

Implementing Health Education Programs

Competency B
Infer enabling objectives as needed to implement instructional programs
in specified settings.

Sub-Competency 1
Pretest learners to ascertain present abilities and knowledge relative to proposed
program objectives.

<u>Activity: Writing A Pretest On Acquaintance Rape</u>

Student Outcome: The student can develop a knowledge pretest on the topic of acquaintance
rape.

Directions:

1.   Use acquaintance rape as the topic of the program or instructional unit.

2.   Consider the following to be your program objectives. Participants will be able to:

     a. define acquaintance rape
     b. discuss the incidence of acquaintance rape on college campuses
     c. identify at least two possible causes of acquaintance rape
     d. name five recommendations for avoiding acquaintance rape
     e. explain two ways to support a survivor of acquaintance rape

3.   Develop a pretest to determine current knowledge on this topic. Develop true-false,
       multiple choice, matching questions, or short answer questions for the pretest.

4.   Administer the pretest to 10 acquaintances (five men and five women), preferably to
       non-health education majors who may be less likely to be knowledgeable of the topic.

Implementing Health Education Programs

Competency B
Infer enabling objectives as needed to implement instructional programs
in specified settings.

Sub-Competency 2
Develop subordinate measurable objectives as needed for instruction.

Activity: "Enabling" The Learner

Student Outcome: The student can develop enabling objectives and explain the function of those objectives in relationship to general objectives.

Directions:

1.   Check Glossary of Terms at the end of this chapter for definitions of "*general objective*" and "*enabling objective*."

2.   In class, divide into groups of three or four (try to keep School Health students together as well as Community Health). If the group is comprised of School Health majors, select a topic area suitable for a two week unit. If Community Health, select a topic suitable for a seminar series, such as through a hospital. Each group should write five or six "general objectives" for that unit or seminar series.

3.   Under each general objective, brainstorm what health content or skills each learner must have in order to achieve the general objectives.

4.   Practice write several "enabling objectives" for each general objective.

5.   In the groups, discuss the function of enabling objectives in carrying out education programs.

Implementing Health Education Programs

Competency B
Infer enabling objectives as needed to implement instructional programs
in specified settings.

Sub-Competency 2
Develop subordinate measurable objectives as needed for instruction.

Activity: Acquaintance Rape Pretest: Part II

Student Outcome: The student can analyze the acquaintance rape pretest results and add
objectives as needed.

Directions:

1.   Analyze the knowledge pretest results from the activity, "Writing a Pretest on
      Acquaintance Rape" (p. 130).

2.   Determine areas of deficiency for which no measurable objectives were originally
      established as the acquaintance rape program objectives.

3.   Add objectives and content to the instructional program to remedy the knowledge
      deficiency(ies). If need be, revise or add learning activities to meet the objectives.

Implementing Health Education Programs

Competency C
Select methods and media best suited to implement program plans for specific learners.

Sub-Competency 1
Analyze learner characteristics, legal aspects, feasibility, and other considerations influencing choices among methods.

Activity: Activating Each Intelligence

Student Outcome: The student can differentiate among learning preferences as identified in the theory of *multiple intelligences*.

Directions:

1.   Read a minimum of three current articles on the "theory of multiple intelligences."

2.   List the seven distinct ways (multiple intelligences) that we learn and know about reality by naming the seven different intelligences. Provide a short explanation for each of the seven intelligences by using key descriptors or phrases.

3.   Determine which of the seven intelligences are most often activated in health education to help the learner come to know content and skills.

4.   Select three of the remaining intelligences that are not usually activated with methods chosen by the health educator.

5.   For one of the three intelligences selected in step four, develop a learning activity for either a weight management program or drug prevention program.

6.   Try the activity out with classmates and discuss their reactions to using the chosen intelligence for learning.

Getting Started

Consider reading works by Thomas Armstrong, Howard Gardner, David Lazear, or R. G. Sternberg on "multiple intelligences."

Armstrong, T. (1987). In their own way. Los Angeles: J. P. Tarcher.

Armstrong, T. (1993). Seven kinds of smart: Identifying and developing your many intelligences. New York: Penguin.

Armstrong, T. (1994). Multiple intelligences in the classroom. Alexandria, VA: Association for Supervision and Curriculum Development.

Gardner, H. (1991). <u>Multiple intelligences: The theory in practice.</u> New York: Basic Books.

Lazear, D. (1993). <u>Seven pathways of learning: Teaching students and parents about multiple intelligences.</u> Tucson, AZ: Zephr.

Lazear, D. (1993). <u>Seven pathways of knowing: Teaching for multiple intelligences.</u> Palatine, IL: Skylight.

Sternberg, R. G. (1984). <u>Beyond I.Q.: A triarchic theory of human intelligence.</u> New York: Cambridge University Press.

Implementing Health Education Programs

Competency C
Select methods and media best suited to implement program plans for specific learners.

Sub-Competency 1
Analyze learner characteristics, legal aspects, feasibility, and other considerations influencing choices among methods.

Activity: Learning Styles

Student Outcome: The student can identify the difference among various styles of learning.

Directions:

1.   Find at least two articles or sources on "learning styles." Refer to "Getting Started" for some help.

2.   Complete the chart below with the information you have gathered:

LEARNING STYLES

Style Name or Type of Learner	Traits
1. Global	Learn concept then details
2.	
3.	
4.	

3.   Suggest a learning activity for each one of the learning styles listed above.

Getting Started

Dunn, R., & Dunn, K. (1992). Teaching elementary students through their individual learning styles. Boston: Allyn and Bacon.

Klavas, A. (1992). Teaching health education through students' individual learning styles: Strengthening health education for the 1990s. Reston, VA: Association for the Advancement of Health Education.

O'Neil, J. (1990). Making sense of style. Educational Leadership, 47 (2), 5-6.

Implementing Health Education Programs

Competency C
Select methods and media best suited to implement program plans for specific learners.

Sub-Competency 2
Evaluate the efficacy of alternative methods and techniques capable of facilitating program objectives.

Activity: A Checklist For Evaluating Program Interventions

Student Outcome: The student can develop a checklist for the purpose of applying criteria to evaluate *interventions*.

Directions:

1.   Listed below are some criteria for designing effective health promotion interventions:

* addresses one or more risk factors of the target group.
* is appropriate for the learning styles, special characteristics, needs, and
   preferences of the target group.
* is appropriate for available resources.
* is appropriate for the types of objectives developed for the program.

2.   Using the four criteria above, develop a checklist that could be used to evaluate the appropriateness and effectiveness of interventions.

Getting Started

Two documents that address the criteria for designing interventions are:

Ad Hoc Work Group of the American Public Health Association. (1987). Criteria for the development of health promotion and education programs. American Journal of Public Health, 77, 89-92.

National Center for Chronic Disease Prevention and Health Promotion. (1995). Planned approach to community health: Guide for local coordinators. Atlanta, GA: Centers for Disease Control.

Implementing Health Education Programs

Competency C
Select methods and media best suited to implement program plans for specific learners.

Sub-Competency 2
Evaluate the efficacy of alternative methods and techniques capable of facilitating program objectives.

Activity: Doing The Right Thing

Student Outcome: The student can evaluate a variety of methods according to their efficacy of facilitating cognitive, affective, or skill-building objectives.

Directions:

1.   Place each of the methods listed on the bottom of this page in the column under the objective type that the particular method would most likely facilitate objective achievement.

TYPES OF OBJECTIVES

Cognitive	Affective	Skill-building (Performance)

Audiotapes	Guest Speaker	Self-appraisals
Audiovisual aids	Lecture	Simulation
Brainstorming	Mass media	Word puzzles/games
Demonstration	Music	
Discussion	Personal improvement projects	
Experiment	Reading	
Field Trips	Role Play	

2.   Include any additional methods not identified on the list.

3.   Asterisk methods that may facilitate the achievement of two or more objective types. Be sure to include the method in additional column(s).

4.   Write three objectives, including a cognitive, affective, and skill-based program objective, for a community health education program with a focus on radon as a potential health problem.

5.   Identify one method to achieve each of the three stated objectives, then explain why it would be a better choice than others in the same column.

Implementing Health Education Programs

Competency C
Select methods and media best suited to implement program plans for specific learners.

Sub-Competency 3
Determine the availability of information, personnel, time, and equipment needed to implement the program for a given audience.

Activity: Mastering A Media Blitz

Student Outcome: The student can determine the availability of media channels and outlets for use in a media blitz for a sun protection program for caregivers of children and youth.

Directions:

1.   A month long media blitz on ultraviolet ray protection is being planned for reaching caregivers of children and youth in a metropolitan area.

2.   Determine the types of media that will be used to reach the target audience. Examples include newspaper ads, press releases, public service announcements (PSA), feature articles, and billboards.

3.   Call local radio and television stations to seek information on free air time and requirements for submitting a PSA. Requirements will vary according to length of PSA, number of days or weeks station must have material, format of PSA, and the title of the person to whom it is sent.

4.   Identify types of media in the community who should receive a press release for a kick-off event that involves a dermatologist speaking to local area daycare personnel or parents.

5.   Identify who should be contacted for guidelines on submission of a feature article for the local newspaper on sun protection for children and youth.

6.   Locate a local billboard or marquee and investigate how to get a message on it, costs involved, time period for promotional message, and specific requirements for use.

7.   Check on costs of newspaper advertising.

8.   Determine total length of time spent on media blitz preparation as well as approximate costs for promoting program via media.

Implementing Health Education Programs

Competency C
Select methods and media best suited to implement program plans for specific learners.

Sub-Competency 3
Determine the availability of information, personnel, time, and equipment needed to implement the program for a given audience.

Activity: Material Selection Analysis

Student Outcome: The student can compare the advantages and disadvantages of developing in-house instructional materials or purchasing existing packaged programs.

Directions:

1.   You are in charge of selecting the instructional materials to be used in a community blood pressure awareness program. You are undecided as to whether you should develop in-house materials or purchase a program from a commercial vendor or non-profit agency.

2.   Research or brainstorm a list of advantages and disadvantages for in-house materials and packaged programs using the charts on the next page.

Getting Started

Contact local voluntary health agencies, local hospitals, or the public health departments for information on materials and programs they may have available.

MATERIAL SELECTION ANALYSIS

	Advantages	Disadvantages
In-House Material Development		

	Advantages	Disadvantages
Purchase of Packaged Program		

Notes

Implementing Health Education Programs

Competency D
Monitor educational programs, adjusting objectives and activities as necessary.

Sub-Competency 1
Compare actual program activities with the stated objectives.

Activity: Correlation Of Program Activities With Stated Objectives

Student Outcome: The student can evaluate and select appropriate instructional activities to be used in achieving program objectives.

Directions:

1.   Choose five objectives written for the activity, "Developing a Framework of Program Objectives" (p. 81).

2.   Obtain copies of sources containing instructional activities for health education. Examples of such sources are provided in the "Getting Started" section below.

3.   Identify 3-5 instructional activities for each of the five objectives chosen. Record the source of each activity.

4.   Review each activity. Through revision or elimination of activities, choose one activity best suited to achieving each specific objective. Justify your choices.

Getting Started

Greenberg, J. S. (1995). Health education learner-centered instructional strategies (3rd ed.). Dubuque, IA: Wm. C. Brown.

Meeks, L., & Heit, P. (1992). Comprehensive school health education: Totally awesome strategies for teaching health. Blacklick, OH: Meeks and Heit.

Meeks, L., Heit, P., & Burt, J. (1993). Education for sexuality and HIV/AIDS: Curriculum and teaching strategies. Blacklick, OH: Meeks and Heit.

Meeks, L., Heit, P., & Page, R. (1995). Violence prevention: Totally awesome teaching strategies for safe and drug-free schools. Blacklick, OH: Meeks and Heit.

Tillman, K. G., & Rizzo, P. (1990). How to survive teaching health: Games, activities, and worksheets for grades 4-12. West Nyack, NY: Parker.

Implementing Health Education Programs

Competency D
Monitor educational programs, adjusting objectives and activities as necessary.

Sub-Competency 1
Compare actual program activities with the stated objectives.

<u>Activity: Revising Activities As Necessary</u>

Student Outcome: The student can develop possible solutions when confronted with a need to alter or eliminate certain program activities.

Directions:

1.   With a partner, brainstorm at least five reasons why activities planned for an educational program might need to be revised or eliminated. Consider all possible reasons, such as time, equipment problems, or abilities of participants. Record your ideas in the chart provided.

2.   Now work with your partner to develop solutions for each reason. Be creative; some factors may have more than one alternative solution. What aspects of your program would you revise? What would you eliminate?

3.   Justify your reasoning for the solutions suggested.

REVISING ACTIVITIES AS NECESSARY

Possible Factors   Possible Solutions

1. Activity too elementary for   1. Eliminate activity. Revise it between
    participants.   sessions to make it more challenging.

2.   2.

3.   3.

4.   4.

Justification for solutions:

Notes

Implementing Health Education Programs

Competency D
Monitor educational programs, adjusting objectives and activities as necessary.

Sub-Competency 2
Assess the relevance of existing program objectives to current needs.

Activity: Using "CAT" Successfully

Student Outcome: The student can utilize an effective but quick assessment technique to identify whether health content or skills are being understood by participants.

Directions:

1.   During the implementation of a program or lesson, it is important to check how well the objectives are being met. One method of doing this is utilization of "CAT" or Classroom Assessment Techniques. For example, during a break in a program or class, ask participants to write down the three main ideas or concepts they have learned so far. Another variation is to request participants to write down the concept or idea that is confusing or not well understood. Information received can be used in subsequent classes or sessions to review ideas or present material in different ways.

2.   In many health education courses, you will be asked to give an oral presentation. Next time, take one or two minutes at the end of your presentation to conduct a "CAT."

Getting Started

Angelo, T. A., & Cross, K. P. (1993). Classroom assessment techniques: A handbook for college teachers (2nd ed.). San Francisco, CA: Jossey-Bass.

Implementing Health Education Programs

Competency D
Monitor educational programs, adjusting objectives and activities as necessary.

Sub-Competency 2
Assess the relevance of existing program objectives to current needs.

Activity: Cut, Adjust Or Keep

Student Outcome: The student can identify ways to assess the relevance of an existing program.

Directions:

1.   Review the following objectives of a college peer education program implemented three years ago. The program focus has been prevention of sexual assault among college students. Objectives include:

* Increase awareness of sexual assault on campus
* Increase recognition of potential high risk situations involving sexual assault
* Train female college students in the skills of self-protection
* Reduce the incidence of sexual assault on campus

2.   The program, two one hour sessions, has been given to members of resident halls, sororities, and campus organizations/clubs. Several programs have been delivered each of the three past years.

3.   During an annual review of the college peer education programs, it is determined the interest in the sexual assault prevention program is declining. What kinds of information will be needed to determine the current relevance of the program and the need to maintain offering it in the future? How would this information be obtained? For example, contact may be made with campus police to obtain records on numbers of sexual assaults in the past year. Current data may then be compared to data of previous years.

Implementing Health Education Programs

Competency D
Monitor educational programs, adjusting objectives and activities as necessary.

Sub-Competency 3
Revise program activities and objectives as necessitated by changes in learner needs.

Activity: Language of The Learner

Student Outcome: The student can identify program modifications for multicultural populations.

Directions:

1.   Read the Cardio Plus activity for descriptive information on the Cardio Plus Program (p. 71).

2.   During a recent review of the Cardio Plus Program, it was noted that the demographic make-up of the program participants had changed. The major change was that almost one-third of the new participants are Hispanic and speak English as their second language. In addition, most Hispanic participants have indicated a preference for materails written in Spanish.

3.   Identify ways the health educator could make changes in the program to accommodate the increasing number of Hispanic participants. For example, the health educator may have the monthly program newsletter written in both English and Spanish versions.

Getting Started

Check with agencies providing heart health information regarding availability of reading materials in different languages.

Implementing Health Education Programs

Competency D
Monitor educational programs, adjusting objectives and activities as necessary.

Sub-Competency 3
Revise program activities and objectives as necessitated by changes in learner needs.

<u>Activity: Revising Objectives During Program Implementation</u>

Student Outcome: The student can utilize data collected from learners to revise original program objectives.

Directions:

1.   Imagine that you are presenting an educational program on tobacco issues and adolescents. Imagine also that the six program objectives listed below were the objectives used to develop the program. At the end of the first day or session, you administer a brief evaluation form to see how the program is meeting the learners' needs. The data indicate the learners are very interested in the following topics:

* smokeless tobacco
* cessation techniques
* laws concerning access to tobacco by minors

2.   The data also reveal that learners feel very knowledgeable already about the following topics:

* physical health problems associated with tobacco
* indoor tobacco-free environment laws

3.   Based on this information, revise the following program objectives:

a.   The participant will be able to identify the five most common reasons why adolescents begin to use tobacco products.

b.   The participant will be able to recognize and define the most common types of tobacco advertising that appeal to younger people.

c.   The participant will be able to list and define the five most serious health problems related to use of tobacco products.

d.   The participant will be able to describe the psychological and physical addictive process associated with use of tobacco products.

e. The participant will be able to explain current federal laws concerning use of tobacco products in public areas.

f. The participant will be able to identify the most successful smoking cessation techniques.

Implementing Health Education Programs

Competency D
Monitor educational programs, adjusting objectives and activities as necessary.

Sub-Competency 4
Appraise applicability of resources and materials relative to given educational objectives.

<u>Activity: Evaluating The Appropriateness Of Resources</u>

Student Outcome: The student can identify potential resources and materials that are appropriate to the objectives of a program. In addition, the student can evaluate that resource based on pre-established criteria.

Directions:

1.   Select a health topic in which you have some background knowledge. Use a topic that would be appropriate for one class or program. For example, select "eating disorders," not the larger subject of nutrition. Select also a target population such as high school students or elders.

2.   Utilizing your background knowledge, write two or three content (cognitive) objectives.

3.   List three reliable health-related sources where you might obtain appropriate educational materials.

4.   Actually obtain one example of identified materials, whether it be a pamphlet, video, fact sheet, etc.

5.   Evaluate this material based on criteria you have selected. On what basis would you include or eliminate this resource? For example, is the readability level appropriate for your target population? Is print size appropriate for audience?

6.   On a one page sheet to be turned into the instructor, list topic, sample objectives, possible resources, and criteria for evaluating materials. Attach the selected educational resource to the paper with justification for selection or elimination.

Implementing Health Education Programs

Competency D
Monitor educational programs, adjusting objectives and activities as necessary.

Sub-Competency 4
Appraise applicability of resources and materials relative to given educational objectives.

Activity: Information And Materials Search

Student Outcome: The student can identify and evaluate educational materials and sources of information appropriate for specific target groups in a worksite cardiovascular risk reduction program.

Directions:

1.   Choose three of the six content areas identified in the activity, "Cardio Plus Program" (p. 71), to be used in this activity.

2.   Identify sources of health-related information applicable to those three content areas.

3.   Evaluate the appropriateness of the health-related information and educational materials for the various employee target groups (e.g., gender, age, heart-health status, etc.) noted in the "Cardio Plus Program" activity.

Notes

Glossary of Terms

enabling factors: skills or resources necessary for a desired behavior to occur

enabling objectives: objectives that provide the skills and knowledge for every learner to be at the same point of readiness

experiential: derived from past experiences or providing current experiences

general objectives: statements that outline the general steps required to meet a specified goal

implementation: the strategic plan for putting a program into action

intervention: the experiences or activities that the program participants are exposed to in order to meet the objectives

multiple intelligences: a theory of understanding human intelligence in which there are at least seven different ways of learning, as opposed to the idea that intelligence is a single, static measurement

Notes

References

Ames, E., Trucano, L., Wan, J., & Harris, M. (1995). <u>Designing school health curricula.</u> Dubuque, IA: Brown and Benchmark.

Dignan, M. B., & Carr, P. A. (1992). <u>Program planning for health education and promotion.</u> Philadelphia: Lea and Febiger.

Green, L. W., & Krueter, M. W. (1991). <u>Health promotion and planning: An educational and environmental approach</u> (2nd ed.). Palo Alto, CA: Mayfield.

McKenzie, J. F., & Smeltzer, J. L. (1997). <u>Planning, implementing, and evaluating health promotion programs: A primer</u> (2nd ed.). Boston: Allyn and Bacon.

National Commission for Health Education Credentialing, Inc. (1996). <u>A competency-based framework for professional development of certified health education specialists.</u> Allentown, PA: Author.

National Task Force on the Preparation and Practice of Health Educators, Inc. (1985). <u>A framework for the development of competency-based curricula for entry-level health educators.</u> New York: Author.

Parkinson, R.S., & Associates. (1982). <u>Managing health promotion in the workplace: Guidelines for implementation and evaluation.</u> Palo Alto, CA: Mayfield.

Ross, H. S., & Mico, P. R. (1980). <u>Theory and practice in health education.</u> Palo Alto, CA: Mayfield.

Timmreck, T. C. (1995). <u>Planning, program development, and evaluation: A handbook for health promotion, aging, and health services.</u> Boston: Jones and Bartlett.

Notes

4.   *Evaluating the Effectiveness of Health Education Programs*

Was the program effective? This question provides the impetus for the health educator in planning the program evaluation. One definition of evaluation refers to it as "the process of determining the degree to which an objective of a program or procedure has been completed or met" (Timmreck, 1995, p. 180). There are many reasons to evaluate a program including, but not limited to, the following:

1.   To determine program effectiveness

2.   To assess achievement of goals and objectives

3.   To identify strengths and weaknesses of the program

4.   To provide information about the implementation process

5.   To be accountable to funding agencies

6.   To assess cost effectiveness

Regardless of the reason behind the evaluation, it must be part of the planning process. The focus and scope of the evaluation should be decided upon in the early phases of program development to provide feedback before, during, and after the program (Muraskin, 1993; Simons-Morton, Greene, & Gottlieb, 1995). The evaluation plan consists of several components: the standards of performance, the level of evaluation, the data collection methods, data analysis, interpretation of the results, and reporting of the results.

The standards of performance relate to the criteria set to judge the program's effectiveness or success. These are usually established within the objectives of the program if the objectives are comprehensive and written clearly. For example, in Chapter 2, a series of objectives were developed for a diabetic education program (page 75). One of the objectives read, "after completing a health risk survey, 80% of the participants will be able to identify their personal risk factors for developing health problems associated with their diabetes." The standard of performance for that objective is "80%" of the participants.

Three levels of evaluation commonly used in health education program planning are *process*, *impact*, and *outcome* (Green & Kreuter, 1991). Process evaluation "describes and assesses program materials and activities" (Muraskin, 1993, p. 5). Activities associated with the administration and implementation of the program are considered in the process evaluation. Information is gathered on things such as the availability of resources (funds, personnel, time, space), appropriateness of the materials used in the program, the ability of the program to reach its intended audience, participant satisfaction with their experiences, and qualifications of the instructors. Methods commonly used to gather this information include questionnaires, monitoring things such as timetables and budgets to determine if deadlines are being met and expenses are within established limits, record keeping, participant interviews and observations, participant self-reports, logs or diaries (Green & Kreuter, 1991; McKenzie & Smeltzer, 1997; Pirie, 1990; Simons-Morton, Greene, & Gottlieb, 1995).

Impact evaluation focuses on the immediate or direct effects of the program on the participants' knowledge, attitudes, and behaviors. At another level, impact evaluation might address the influence of the program on an organization's policies, resources, and activities. Lastly, impact evaluation might investigate the influence of the program on government policies, plans, funding, or legislation (Dignan & Carr, 1992; Muraskin, 1993; Simons-Morton, Greene, & Gottlieb, 1995). Methods used to gather impact evaluation data include post tests to determine changes in knowledge or attitudes, exit interviews, and short-term follow-up questionnaires or interviews to possibly assess changes in behavior.

Outcome evaluation "determines whether the program met the stated long-term goals and objectives" (McKenzie & Smeltzer, 1997, p. 225). Improvements in health and social factors and the quality of life over time are measured at this evaluation level. Information is collected through follow-up questionnaires and interviews, examination of morbidity and mortality rates to determine changes in the death rates or prevalence of certain illness, and review of hospital, public health, or physician visit records to determine differences or changes in use patterns (McKenzie & Smeltzer, 1997; Timmreck, 1995; National Cancer Institute, 1992).

Once the evaluation information is collected, appropriate data analysis will need to be performed to allow the planners to interpret results, draw conclusions about the success of the program, and make recommendations for future program changes and planning. These results, conclusions, and recommendations will then need to be communicated to the appropriate audiences. In the next few paragraphs, examples of all three levels of evaluation (process, impact, and outcome) and their use in the various health education settings are explored.

Community Health Setting

The number of alcohol-related crashes is a concern for a particular rural community. To address the problem, a task force puts together a comprehensive prevention program. The question that becomes a focus for the outcome evaluation is, "has the incidence of alcohol-related crashes decreased?" To answer this question, baseline data concerning the rate of crashes prior to the program involving alcohol will be collected from the local police department. Two years after the program is implemented, police reports will again be examined. Crash rates prior to the program will be compared to rates after the program to determine if any differences have occurred and whether the differences are statistically

significant.

Medical Setting

A farm safety and awareness program was implemented by the community health

education department of a local hospital. The evaluation has been completed and the results

analyzed. To communicate the outcomes to the public, the planners develop a plan for

disseminating the results of the evaluation. An article will be written and submitted to a

professional health journal and a summary sent to local professional newsletters as well as the

local newspaper. A poster presentation will be given at a professional meeting. In addition,

the plan includes sending information about the program and sample materials to related

clearinghouses and state agencies. Finally, the written evaluation report will be added to the

hospital's home page on the World Wide Web and a summary sent to subscribers of the

Health Education Directory.

Post-Secondary Setting

To determine the impact of a new intervention on the attitudes of student athletes

concerning anabolic steroids, a pretest-posttest method of evaluation is selected. One group

of athletes will be placed in the *experimental group* and exposed to the intervention during the

"Life Skills Seminars" sponsored by the Athletics Department. Traditional teaching strategies

will be used with another group placed in the *comparison group*. A *bipolar* survey designed

to measure attitudes toward anabolic steroid use will be used as the pretest and posttest. The

chi square test will be used to statistically analyze the results and test the hypothesis.

School Setting

A school district recently made the decision to adopt a drug prevention program aimed

at deterring the use or possession of drugs at school. For the evaluation instrument, the program planners decide to adapt the <u>Monitoring the Future Survey</u> and <u>Youth Risk Behavior Survey</u>. Questions relating to drug use patterns will be selected from each survey and pulled together to form a new questionnaire. As part of the process evaluation plan, the planners will conduct a *pilot test* with the instrument with a sample of students. The pilot test will provide feedback on such things as the length of time needed to complete the questionnaire and the appropriateness of the reading level.

Worksite Setting

A campaign to lower blood pressure is being initiated by the health educator at a local worksite. The campaign involves a variety of strategies to help achieve the program goal and objectives. One objective is to increase the number of employees who stop in the health education resource room to have blood pressure checked. As part of the evaluation plan, the health educator will monitor resource room utilization records during the program. Daily counts of the number of employees requesting blood pressure checks will provide data for the process evaluation.

Evaluating Effectiveness of Health Education Programs

Competency A
Develop plans to assess achievement of program objectives.

Sub-Competency 1
Determine standards of performance to be applied as criteria of effectiveness.

Activity: Evaluation Standards: Asking The Right Questions

Student Outcome: The student can identify four attributes of sound and fair evaluation and determine key questions to be asked before designing the evaluation.

Directions:

1.   The Program Evaluation Standards is a project supported by numerous educational professional associations. Its purpose is to provide a guide for evaluating educational and training programs, projects, and materials in a variety of settings. As defined in this book, there are four attributes of sound and fair evaluation that should be considered when developing an evaluation plan.

2.   In groups of four, read the four attributes of sound and fair evaluation on the next two pages. Discuss the four attributes thoroughly so that each group member has a clear understanding of each.

3.   Now develop four questions for each attribute that should be asked by evaluators as they begin to develop an evaluation plan. An example of a question is provided for each attribute to help each group get started.

Getting Started

Joint Committee on Standards for Educational Evaluation. (1994). The program evaluation standards: How to assess evaluations of educational programs (2nd ed.). Thousand Oaks, CA: Sage.

EVALUATION STANDARDS: ASKING THE RIGHT QUESTIONS

Utility: Standards that guide evaluations so that they will be informative, timely, and influential. They require evaluators to acquaint themselves with their audiences, define the audiences clearly, ascertain the audiences' information needs, plan evaluation to respond to these needs, and report the relevant information clearly and in a timely fashion (Joint Committee on Standards for Educational Evaluation, 1994, p. 5).

Example Questions to be Asked

1.   How soon must the evaluation be completed?

2.

3.

4.

Feasibility: Standards that recognize evaluations usually are conducted in a natural setting, as opposed to a laboratory setting, and consume valuable resources. Therefore, evaluation designs must be operable in field settings, and evaluations must not consume more resources, materials, personnel, or time than necessary to address the evaluation questions (Joint Committee on Standards for Educational Evaluation, 1994, p. 6).

Example Questions to be Asked

1.   How many persons will be needed to effectively conduct the entire evaluation?

2.

3.

4.

EVALUATION STANDARDS: ASKING THE RIGHT QUESTIONS - CON'T.

Propriety: Standards that reflect the fact that evaluations affect many people in a variety of ways. These standards are intended to facilitate protection of the rights of individuals affected by an evaluation. They promote sensitivity to and warn against unlawful, unscrupulous, unethical, and inept actions by those who conduct evaluations (Joint Committee on Standards for Educational Evaluation, 1994, p. 6).

Example Questions to be Asked

1.   Will questionnaires be confidential or anonymous?

2.

3.

4.

Accuracy: Standards that determine whether an evaluation has produced sound information. The evaluation of a program must be comprehensive; that is, the evaluators should have considered as many of the program's identifiable features as practical, and should have gathered data on those particular features judged important for assessing the program's worth or merit. Moreover, the information must be technically adequate, and the judgments rendered must be linked logically to the data (Joint Committee on Standards for Educational Evaluation, 1994, p. 6).

Example Questions to be Asked

1.   Will all measures be quantitative, or will qualitative measures be appropriate?

2.

3.

4.

Evaluating Effectiveness of Health Education Programs

Competency A
Develop plans to assess achievement of program objectives.

Sub-Competency 1
Determine standards of performance to be applied as criteria of effectiveness.

Activity: Identifying Standards Of Acceptability

Student Outcome: The student can identify examples of commonly used standards for evaluating health education/promotion programs using one of the CDC's adolescent risk behavior priority areas.

Directions:

1.   Select one of the Centers for Disease Control and Prevention's six adolescent risk behavior priority areas: tobacco use, dietary patterns, sedentary lifestyles, sexual behaviors, alcohol and other drug use, and behaviors that result in intentional and unintentional injury.

2.   For each standard of acceptability listed on the following practice chart, develop at least one example of potential standards of performance relevant to the priority area you have selected.

Getting Started

        The chart at the top of the next page has an example of each of the standards of acceptability. It may be helpful as you develop your own examples of standards. The chart is adapted from Planning, Implementing, and Evaluating Health Promotion Programs: A Primer (2nd ed.) by McKenzie, J. F., & Smeltzer, J. L. (1997). Boston: Allyn and Bacon. Used by permission of the authors.

Sample Chart for Sedentary Lifestyles

Standard of Acceptability	Examples
Mandate (policies, statutes, laws)	None applicable*
Target population health status	Increase to at least 75% the proportion of children and adolescents who engage in vigorous physical activity that promotes cardiorespiratory fitness
Community values	Daily physical education required in schools
Standards advocated by professional organizations	CDC/American College of Sports Medicine exercise guidelines for health promotion
Norms established via research	Exercise at target pulse rate for at least 30 minutes at least three times per week; Heart Rate Recovery Test
Norms established by previous programs	Physical Activity Readiness Questionnaire (PAR-Q)

*not all standards are applicable for all areas

Practice Chart

Standard of Acceptability	Examples
Mandate of regulating agencies	
Target population health status	
Community values	
Standards advocated by professional organizations	
Norms established via research	
Norms established by previous programs	

Evaluating Effectiveness of Health Education Programs

Competency A
Develop plans to assess achievement of program objectives.

Sub-Competency 2
Establish a realistic scope of evaluation efforts.

<u>Activity: Planning For Evaluation</u>

Student Outcome: The student can demonstrate the ability to develop an evaluation plan of sufficient scope.

Directions:

1.   Using the following purpose, identify the types of evaluation (formative, summative, process, outcome, or impact) you would use to measure the effectiveness of the program.

       Purpose: You want to determine the problem areas in a school-based tobacco prevention program in your district. The goal of "Smoke-Free" is to prevent smoking among junior high school students. Objectives of the program are to: a) educate students of the harmful effects of smoking, b) help students understand peer pressure, and c) teach students effective refusal skills.

2.   Write a paragraph explaining each type of evaluation you plan to use to evaluate the tobacco prevention program.

3.   Look ahead to the activity, "Identifying Evaluation Methods" (p. 178). Use this same example to complete that activity.

Evaluating Effectiveness of Health Education Programs

Competency A
Develop plans to assess achievement of program objectives.

Sub-Competency 2
Establish a realistic scope of evaluation efforts.

<u>Activity:</u> <u>Process, Impact, And Outcome: Which To Include?</u>

Student Outcome: The student can define the three types of program evaluation and describe when and how each is used.

Directions:

1.   The first step in designing an evaluation plan for a health education program is deciding the "scope." For example, are you interested only in the process of program implementation? Are changes in the participants' knowledge, attitudes, or behaviors important aspects of the evaluation plan?

2.   First identify a definition of process, impact, and outcome evaluation. There is a definition of each included in the Glossary of Terms, but check a second source, such as a health education program planning textbook.

3.   On the following worksheet, complete question one to help you understand the types of program evaluation. Answer questions 2 through 7 to help you explore the various uses of evaluation.

<u>Getting Started</u>

See Glossary of Terms at the end of this chapter for definitions of process, outcome, and impact evaluation.

PROCESS, IMPACT, AND OUTCOME: WHICH TO INCLUDE?

1.   For this activity, provide a definition of the three types of program evaluation.
      Include appropriate reference information.

   a. *Process:*

      Reference:

   b. *Impact:*

      Reference:

   c. *Outcome:*

      Reference:

2.   School health education teachers utilize which type of evaluation most often?
      Provide an explanation for your choice.

3.   Hospitals who send out customer satisfaction surveys are using what type of
      evaluation? Provide an explanation for your choice.

PROCESS, IMPACT, AND OUTCOME: WHICH TO INCLUDE? - CON'T.

4.   Six months after a smoking cessation class, the American Lung Association calls participants to find out whether they have continued not to smoke. What type of evaluation is being conducted? Justify your choice.

5.   Which type of evaluation is almost always included in any evaluation plan? Why is that so?

6.   How are impact and outcome evaluations similar? How do they differ?

7.   Long term behavior change is measured by which type of evaluation? What are the barriers to including this type of evaluation?

Evaluating Effectiveness of Health Education Programs

Competency A
Develop plans to assess achievement of program objectives.

Sub-Competency 3
Develop an inventory of existing valid and reliable tests and instruments.

Activity: "Homemade" Instruments: Advantages And Disadvantages

Student Outcome: The student can list the circumstances under which he/she might develop a program evaluation instrument instead of using existing ones.

Directions:

1.   Review definitions of "*reliability*" and "*validity*" to begin this assignment. Check definitions of "process," "impact," and "outcome" evaluations if necessary.

2.   Imagine that you must design and implement an evaluation plan for a health education program being offered by a county health department.

3.   Complete the attached worksheet to compare the advantages and disadvantages of homemade instruments.

Getting Started

The Glossary of Terms at the end of this chapter will provide definitions needed to complete this activity. Also, check your library for this excellent reference:

Scriven, M. (1991). Evaluation thesaurus (4th ed.). Newbury Park, CA: Sage.

Notes

"HOMEMADE" INSTRUMENTS:
ADVANTAGES AND DISADVANTAGES

1.   Describe two circumstances in which a program evaluator might develop his/her own instrument.

      a.

      b.

2.   How are validity and reliability affected by instruments that are "homemade?"

3.   Consider the three types of program evaluation (process, impact, outcome). A homemade instrument might be most appropriate for which type of evaluation? Why?

4.   For which type of evaluation would you be more likely to use instruments that report measures of validity and reliability? Why?

5.   Develop a paragraph describing the advantages and disadvantages of using "homemade" instruments for program evaluation.

Notes

Evaluating Effectiveness of Health Education Programs

Competency A
Develop plans to assess achievement of program objectives.

Sub-Competency 3
Develop an inventory of existing valid and reliable tests and instruments.

Activity: Resource File Of Program Evaluation Instruments

Student Outcome: The student can demonstrate proficiency in locating valid and reliable instruments and surveys.

Directions:

1.   Choose one of the following program topics to research:

* tobacco prevention programs
* exercise promotion programs
* alcohol and drug use prevention programs
* HIV/AIDS and other STD prevention programs
* violence prevention programs
* weight control programs

2.   Locate potential evaluation instruments.

3.   Use 3" x 5" index cards to record the following information:

* name of instrument
* source (where to get a copy)
* reported validity (type and how assessed)
* reported reliability (type and coefficient, if applicable)

Getting Started

Computer databases, reference books, and the Internet might be useful resources to use. You may wish to begin by searching for articles that report results of prevention programs on the topic area chosen. From those articles you might find samples of evaluation instruments or references to such instruments.

Evaluating Effectiveness of Health Education Programs

Competency A
Develop plans to assess achievement of program objectives.

Sub-Competency 4
Select appropriate methods for evaluating program effectiveness.

<u>Activity: Identifying Evaluation Methods</u>

Student Outcome: The student can explain how a variety of evaluation methods can be used in order to achieve a realistic scope of evaluation efforts.

Directions:

1.   Refer to the activity, "Planning for Evaluation" (p. 169), in which you determined types of evaluation that would be used to evaluate the problem areas and weaknesses in the school-based tobacco use prevention effort known as "Smoke-Free."

2.   Describe when and how six of the following methods could be used in the evaluation plan. Choose three from each column:

* assess health status changes   * morbidity and mortality data
    (examine existing records)   * participant observation
* classroom observations   * pilot test
* daily logs   * pre- and post tests
* examine school/community records   * questionnaire
* field testing   * surveys
* focus groups   * tracking forms
* in-depth interviews

Evaluating Effectiveness of Health Education Programs

Competency A
Develop plans to assess achievement of program objectives.

Sub-Competency 4
Select appropriate methods for evaluating program effectiveness.

Activity: Using Qualitative And Quantitative Methods In Program Evaluation

Student Outcome: The student can design a process evaluation plan utilizing both *qualitative* and *quantitative methods*.

Directions:

1. Turn to the Glossary of Terms at the end of the chapter and review the definition of "qualitative methods." Check additional sources as needed for additional clarification. In particular, think about how the purpose of qualitative methods differs from quantitative methods.

2. Imagine that you are a health educator at a county public health department that has implemented a radon awareness program which involved public presentations, distribution of pamphlets at local grocery stores, public service announcements on local radio stations, and press releases to the local newspaper.

Objectives of Radon Awareness Program

   a. Develop an awareness of radon and its possible health hazards.
   b. Encourage community members to seek additional information about radon.
   c. Inform community members as to the various methods/sources for home radon testing.
   d. Encourage community members to test homes for radon.

3. Your supervisor has asked you to develop an evaluation plan involving both quantitative and qualitative methods. She asks you to learn what happened and why.

4. Develop the evaluation plan using the attached worksheet.

Notes

USING QUALITATIVE AND QUANTITATIVE METHODS IN PROGRAM EVALUATION

Program Objective	Type of Evaluation Method	Quantitative	Qualitative
(Example) a. Develop an awareness of radon and its possible health hazards.	Distribute pamphlets at local grocery stores for a two-month period.	✓	
b. Encourage community members to seek additional information about radon.			
c. Inform community members as to the various methods/sources for home radon testing.			
d. Encourage community members to test homes for radon.			

Notes

Evaluating Effectiveness of Health Education Programs

Competency B
Carry out evaluation plans.

Sub-Competency 1
Facilitate administration of the tests and activities specified in the plan.

Activity: GANG Violence Prevention Program Evaluation

Student Outcome: The student can explain how to implement an evaluation plan.

Directions:

1.   A group of five concerned community members have gathered to evaluate the "Gangs Are Not Good" (GANG) Violence Prevention Program. Following is a description of the information gathered to date.

With the help of a hired professional evaluator, three of the five committee members are willing to conduct the program evaluation (a former gang member, a police officer, and a teacher). A budget involving $2000 has been developed. The use of two instruments has been suggested: a) a written survey with forced choice and open-ended questions, and b) focus group interviews of gang member participants. A time-line for conducting the evaluation has been created.

2.   With this information, answer the following questions:

a. Who is responsible for developing the written survey and the questions for the focus group interviews?
b. Who will be responsible for collecting the data using 1) the written survey, and 2) the focus group interview format?
c. How, when, and where will the data be collected?
d. Will the whole sample of participants or a random sample be included in the evaluation?
e. Who will analyze the data?
f. Who will receive the results?
g. Who will report the results?
h. In what form will the results be disseminated?

3.   Justify your decisions for the above assignment of tasks. Discuss the implications of your choices and any potential problems or concerns relating to the evaluation of this program.

Evaluating Effectiveness of Health Education Programs

Competency B
Carry out evaluation plans.

Sub-Competency 1
Facilitate administration of the tests and activities specified in the plan.

<u>Activity: Measurement Versus Evaluation</u>

Student Outcome: The student can differentiate between measurement and evaluation.

Directions:

1.   Look up definitions of the terms "measurement" and "evaluation" from a variety of sources.

2.   Complete the chart below.

	Definition	*Source*
Evaluation		
Evaluation		
Measurement		
Measurement		

3.   Select a "setting" from the introduction to this chapter. In your own words, apply the definitions of measurement and evaluation to the examples used in the setting you have selected.

Evaluating Effectiveness of Health Education Programs

Competency B
Carry out evaluation plans.

Sub-Competency 2
Utilize data collection methods appropriate to the objectives.

Activity: Designing An Evaluation Activity

Student Outcome: The student can devise an evaluation activity that can be used to assess the understanding of subject matter specified in the objectives.

Directions:

1.   Refer to the activity, "Levels of Program Objectives" (page 81). Select one of these objectives or one that you developed for this assignment. (*Hint:* The first attempt at this will be easier if you select one of the first 3 or 4 objectives; i.e., Awareness, Knowledge, Attitudes, or Skills.)

2.   Devise an evaluation activity to assess the subject matter specified in the objective you have selected. See the following example:

Objective: After listening to a lecture on diabetic complications, participants will list three out of five common health problems experienced by diabetics.

Subject Matter Specified in Objective: Common health problems of diabetics.

Evaluation Activity: Test participants' knowledge of program content by asking them to read a scenario and respond to several open-ended questions. An example of the scenario and questions are presented below:

> *Scenario: Three diabetics are having a discussion concerning some problems in their lives. Diabetic number one has been hospitalized on several occasions for high blood sugar levels. He claims to have a hard time monitoring blood sugar, and cannot get to the doctor frequently enough to have it monitored on a regular basis. Diabetic number two complains that he has had to give up reading certain newspapers and magazines because the print has changed and he has a difficult time seeing it. Diabetic number three is having frequent leg cramping and feels tired all the time. Since the cold weather has set in, he no longer goes for his morning walks.*

Please respond to these questions*:*
* What could diabetic number one do, or where could he/she got to have his/her blood sugar monitored on a more regular basis?
* What eye problem should diabetic number two be concerned about? What should he/she do right away?
* What does diabetic number three need to start doing again? What suggestions do you have for this person?

Notes

DESIGNING AN EVALUATION ACTIVITY

Objective:

Subject matter specified in objective:

Evaluation Activity:

Notes

Evaluating Effectiveness of Health Education Programs

Competency B
Carry out evaluation plans.

Sub-Competency 2
Utilize data collection methods appropriate to the objectives.

<u>Activity: "Got A Match?"</u>

Student Outcome: The student can create evaluation activities appropriate to measuring developed program objectives.

Directions:

1.   You have been asked to develop a program on a topic of your choice for the local paper factory employees. Choose a health topic for which you will develop objectives for the program. Topics may include cardiovascular health, stress management, or workplace safety.

2.   Develop one objective for each of the following levels:

* Awareness
* Knowledge
* Attitude
* Skill Development

3.   Briefly explain how each objective will be evaluated, and provide specific examples of the evaluation procedures.

Evaluating Effectiveness of Health Education Programs

Competency B
Carry out evaluation plans.

Sub-Competency 3
Analyze resulting evaluation data.

Activity: Statistical Analysis Of Data

Student Outcome: The student can describe and demonstrate methods involved in statistical analysis of data.

Directions:

1.   Define the following terms:

        * mean   * range
        * median   * standard deviation
        * mode

2.   Using the data set provided, compute the mean, median, mode, range, and standard deviation.

Number of Cigarettes Smoked Daily Over One Month

Day	#	Day	#	Day	#
1	22	11	13	21	7
2	22	12	15	22	7
3	23	13	14	23	5
4	20	14	13	24	5
5	20	15	12	25	4
6	15	16	12	26	4
7	15	17	10	27	3
8	15	18	10	28	0
9	15	19	9	29	1
10	14	20	9	30	1

3.   Describe what this statistical analysis of data means to the participants, program objectives, and program planner.

Evaluating Effectiveness of Health Education Programs

Competency B
Carry out evaluation plans.

Sub-Competency 3
Analyze resulting evaluation data.

Activity: Use Of Computers In Evaluation

Student Outcome: The student can identify software suitable for statistical analysis of evaluation data.

Directions:

1.   Research various types of computer software programs that are designed to assist with statistical analysis of data.

2.   Complete the chart below with the information you gather.

Title	Vendor	Price	Notes

Evaluating Effectiveness of Health Education Programs

Competency C
Interpret results of program evaluation.

Sub-Competency 1
Apply criteria of effectiveness to obtaining results of a program.

Activity: Criteria For Program Effectiveness

Student Outcome: The student can apply a set of criteria to results of an implemented health education program.

Directions:

1.   Read the following set of objectives developed for a two session bicycle safety program targeted toward parents and children in a rural community.

    Session One (Parents)
    a. Interpret national, state, and local statistics of bicycle injuries and fatalities of all age groups.
    b. Describe benefits of proper and consistent use of wearing a bicycle helmet.
    c. Compare and contrast different types of children, youth, and adult bicycle helmets.
    d. Identify sources for purchase of bicycle helmets and other personal bicycle safety equipment.
    e. Observe proper fitting and wearing of a bicycle helmet plus proper procedures for bicycle operation and maintenance.
    f. Value the use of bicycle helmets for safer bicycle operation.

    Session Two (Children)
    g. Explain the effectiveness of a bicycle helmet through observing the demonstration of the Egg Helmet Kit.
    h. Participate in a free bicycle safety check.
    i. Demonstrate knowledge and skills of safe bicycle operation during a bicycle rodeo.
    j. Be aware of the proper personal safety equipment for riding a bicycle.

2.   Through comparing post instructional knowledge, attitudes, and skills to pretest scores, one may make an evaluative judgment on the effectiveness of the bicycle safety program. To facilitate this process, using the above stated program objectives, develop one pretest question in each of the areas of knowledge, skills, and attitudes for adult participants.

3.   In a similar fashion, write pretest questions for the stated objectives for the children, one in the area of knowledge, another in the area of skill, and another in the area of attitude.

4.   Next, determine the different types of criteria that could be established for measuring program effectiveness. One type of criteria may be identified in terms of the "acceptable percent of participants scoring higher on the post scores." For example, a criteria indicating program success may be that 90 percent of all adult participants have post scores higher than pretest scores. A second type of criteria may be identified in terms of an "acceptable percentage of correct or preferred post test responses to any given question." Use the pretest questions written in step three to identify types of acceptable and unacceptable criteria for post scores of the adults and children participating in the bicycle safety program.

5.   Finally, are there other types of criteria that may be established before program implementation that would help to determine program effectiveness? The following questions may help you think about other criteria to be applied to compare desired or acceptable results with actual results:

a. Will the number of participants attending the program be a measure of success? If so, how will such a number be determined?
b. Will the criteria for acceptable post score scores in certain areas, such as knowledge, skills, and attitudes, differ from one another? Why or why not?
c. Will desired changes in pretest and post scores be sufficient criteria for measuring program success? If not, what other criteria can be established for measuring program effectiveness?

6.   Share ideas and justifications for selected criteria with others. Note areas of agreement and disagreement regarding criteria which may be applied to obtain results of a program.

Evaluating Effectiveness of Health Education Programs

Competency C
Interpret results of program evaluation.

Sub-Competency 1
Apply criteria of effectiveness to obtaining results of a program.

Activity: Is It Statistically Significant?

Student Outcome: The student can identify and explain basic statistical terms and procedures used in the evaluation of programs or activities.

Directions:

1.   Find at least two articles in professional journals that utilize a "pretest" and posttest" design to evaluate a program, activity, or project.

2.   Complete the following items:
        * Article Reference:
          a)

          b)

        * Methodology Used (design of study):
          a)

          b)

        * Type of Statistic Used:
          a)

          b)

        * Brief Summary of Results:
          a)

          b)

3.   Define fidelity. Was the term used in either article? ___ yes   ___ no

4.   Define statistical significance. Was the term used in either article? ___ yes   ___ no

Evaluating Effectiveness of Health Education Programs

Competency C
Interpret results of program evaluation.

Sub-Competency 2
Translate evaluation results into terms easily understood by others.

<u>Activity: Charting Progress</u>

Student Outcome: The student can present evaluation findings in the form of graphs, charts, and tables.

Directions:

1.   Access a computer software program designed for presentation of information. Some examples include: Freelance, Harvard Graphics, WordPerfect Presentations, or Persuasion.

2.   Using the two sets of evaluation results provided, organize the findings on the following page in the following ways:

      * Pie Chart
      * Line Graph
      * Bar Graph
      * Table

3.   Write a brief explanation of how the chart, graphs, and table would be explained in an understandable, non-technical manner.

ESTIMATED NEW CANCER CASES
USA - 1996

Male

Prostate	317,100
Lung	98,900
Colon & Rectum	67,600
Bladder	38,300
Lymphoma	33,900
Melanoma of the Skin	21,800
Oral	20,100
Kidney	18,500
Leukemia	15,300
Stomach	14,000
Pancreas	12,400
Liver	10,800
All Sites	764,300

Female

Breast	184,300
Lung	78,100
Colon & Rectum	65,900
Corpus Uteri & Unspecified	34,000
Ovary	26,700
Lymphoma	26,300
Melanoma of the Skin	16,500
Cervix Uteri	15,700
Bladder	14,600
Pancreas	13,900
Leukemia	12,300
Kidney	12,100
All Sites	594,850

Source: American Cancer Society. (1996). <u>Cancer facts and figures - 1996.</u> Atlanta, GA: Author.

Evaluating Effectiveness of Health Education Programs

Competency C
Interpret results of program evaluation.

Sub-Competency 2
Translate evaluation results into terms easily understood by others.

<u>Activity: Graphs For Sharing Evaluation Results</u>

Student Outcome: The student can translate evaluation findings into various graphic formats that allow for easily interpreted results.

Directions:

1.   Review the composite findings of the evaluation results from 22 participants attending an Alzheimer's support program consisting of monthly meetings for a six month period.

Alzheimer's Community Caregivers Support Group
Semi-Annual Evaluation (Responses = 22)

Directions: Please circle the response that most nearly describes your assessment for questions 1 - 6. For questions 7 - 10, use the space provided for your comments. On the reverse side, please provide information about yourself.

	Excellent	Good	Fair	Poor
1. Overall value of this support group	15	4	3	0
2. Meeting facilities	2	11	6	3
3. Format for meetings	9	6	4	2
4. Emotional support offered	16	5	1	0
5. Practical suggestions/ideas	20	2	0	0
6. Special guest speakers	15	5	2	0
7. Materials/resources provided	18	4	0	0

8. The things I liked <u>best</u> about the support group:

   Opportunity to share with others
   Good helpful advice on how to deal with my husband
   Feeling that I am not alone and desperate
   Guest speaker on medications and new drugs under study
   Everything; this has been a wonderful group, especially you, Mrs. Johnson
   Reading material for me to find out more on various subjects
   That others are in the same types of situations and experiencing similar things as me
   All the speakers; they helped me understand areas I wasn't aware of, especially the
      lawyer
   Being able to talk to others with the same feelings and frustrations
   The support I felt from everyone
   Dr. Havermeyer and his information on new drug therapies
   The friends I've made and the information that is so helpful as I struggle to deal with
      providing care for my loved one
   Guest speakers, resources, and friendly atmosphere

9. The things I liked <u>least</u> about the support group:

   Nothing
   Just the place we met; couldn't we find something more conducive to group
      meetings?
   The fact that I couldn't always come on Wednesdays and missed some guest speakers
      I wanted to hear
   Can't think of anything; maybe the room we met in
   The way we heard the same stories from everyone over and over
   Depressing to listen to others with more difficult problems than I now have
   All the time spent listening to others; I just wanted help on how to be a better
      caregiver
   Nothing; great support group--I'm so glad I found you
   Nothing comes to mind
   The room conditions; too hot and noisy most of the time
   My hearing isn't good, and often times I couldn't hear others

10. Recommendations for future meetings:

   Another session on legal issues; it was so helpful
   Better facilities; nice refreshments
   Different times and days of week so I could come; Wednesdays are hard days to find
      a sitter as it is church night
   New room would be great!
   More speakers who are knowledgeable on current research on AD
   Information on adult day care centers and how to choose a nursing home
   Nothing; I've learned so much and like the camaraderie at the meetings

Demographics

Please circle the appropriate response for the following questions.

1. Place of residence?

    _18_ Within the city of XYZ
    _3_ Within 25 miles of XYZ
    _1_ Over 25 miles from XYZ

2. How long have you been caring for a person with Alzheimer's?

    _1_ Less than a year
    _12_ 1-3 years
    _7_ 4-5 years
    _1_ 5-9 years
    _1_ 10 or more years

3. How long have you been participating in our support group?

    _3_ Less than a year
    _14_ 1-2 years
    _3_ 2-3 years
    _2_ Over 3 years

4. How many meetings did you attend so far in 1996?

One	Two	Three	Four	Five	All six meetings
1	2	4	3	4	8

5. How did you learn about this support group?

    _7_ Read about it in the newspaper
    _4_ Heard about it on the radio
    _8_ A friend
    _1_ A medical person
    _2_ Other _____

2. Using the results of the evaluation for the Alzheimer's Support Group Program, determine the best way to display the findings, including the demographics, in graphic format for inclusion in the next newsletter to the participants. Different types of information may be displayed in different formats, such as a pie chart or bar graph. For questions 8-10, determine how to compile the information in a meaningful way for others to read.

3. Complete graphic representations of various findings and share with your classmates and instructor.

Evaluating Effectiveness of Health Education Programs

Competency C
Interpret results of program evaluation.

Sub-Competency 3
Report effectiveness of educational programs in achieving proposed objectives.

<u>Activity: Writing The Report</u>

Student Outcome: The student can report effectiveness of an educational program in achieving proposed objectives in written format.

Directions:

1.   Review the following feedback from 56 participants in a bicycle safety program, and prepare a one page summary of the effectiveness of the program in achieving the proposed objectives. The number of selected participant responses for each objective are in parentheses following each number choice.

Evaluation of Bicycle Safety Program Learner Objectives (Parent Session)

Directions: Please circle the number that best describes the level to which the objective was achieved by you through attending this program. Use the following scale of numbers and their corresponding descriptors:

1 = More than adequately achieved the objective
2 = Adequately achieved the objective
3 = Partially met the objective
4 = Did not achieve the objective

a. Compare national, state, and local statistics of bicycle injuries and fatalities of all age groups.
    1 (8)   2 (48)   3 (0)   4 (0)
b. Describe benefits of proper and consistent use of wearing a bicycle helmet.
    1 (33)   2 (15)   3 (8)   4 (0)
c. Compare and contrast different types of children, youth, and adult bicycle helmets.
    1 (10)   2 (34)   3 (7)   4 (0)
d. Identify sources for purchase of bicycle helmets and other personal bicycle safety equipment.
    1 (0)   2 (17)   3 (38)   4 (1)
e. Observe proper fitting and wearing of a bicycle helmet plus proper procedures for bicycle operation and maintenance.
    1 (29)   2 (22)   3 (4)   4 (0)
f. Value the use of bicycle helmets for safer bike operation by children.
    1 (40)   2 (16)   3 (0)   4 (0)

2.   Prepare a one or two page written narrative for the Board of Directors of the local county health department who sponsored this program. In the report address participants' results for achieving the stated program objectives, and discuss possible reasons for the evaluation results. Also, include in the report a statement or two about the overall effectiveness of the program and provide a rationale for the evaluative judgment made on the program effectiveness.

3.   If you were asked to include graphics with the written narrative, describe what information you would include and the type of graphic format to be used.

Evaluating Effectiveness of Health Education Programs

Competency C
Interpret results of program evaluation.

Sub-Competency 3
Report effectiveness of educational programs in achieving proposed objectives.

<u>Activity: Exploring External Validity</u>

Student Outcome: The student can define external validity/generalizability and explain threats to external validity.

Directions:

1.   Define external validity. Explain how external validity and generalizability are related.

2.   Identify and explain four threats to external validity.

3.   Describe how these threats to external validity can be minimized or counteracted.

4.   Select an evaluation article from the health education literature. Examples of sources include those found in the "Getting Started" section below. Critique the article by focusing on its external validity. Identify any of the above threats encountered in the article. Describe what the author(s) could have done to minimize or counteract these threats.

<u>Getting Started</u>

Articles may be found in the following health education literature sources:

<u>American Journal of Health Behavior</u>
<u>American Journal of Public Health</u>
<u>Health Education Quarterly</u>
<u>The Health Educator</u>
<u>Journal of Health Education</u>
<u>Journal of School Health</u>
<u>Public Health Reports</u>

Evaluating Effectiveness of Health Education Programs

Competency D
Infer implications from findings for future program planning.

Sub-Competency 1
Explore possible explanations for important evaluation findings.

<u>Activity:</u> <u>An Evaluation Is Only As Strong As Its Weaknesses</u>

Student Outcome: The student can identify weaknesses of a commonly used data collection method and explain how the weaknesses may influence the evaluation findings.

Directions:

1.   Select any method used to collect data for program evaluation. Review the partial list in the "Getting Started" section.

2.   Locate several sources on program evaluation. Read about the chosen method.

3.   List the data collection method and define it. Then identify strengths and weaknesses of the method. Finally, write a summary explaining how the weaknesses of the method may affect the data collected for the evaluation.

<u>Getting Started</u>

Commonly used data collection methods:

* Face-to-face interviews
* Focus groups
* Observations
* Questionnaires
* Records
* Telephone interviews

Evaluating Effectiveness of Health Education Programs

Competency D
Infer implications from findings for future program planning.

Sub-Competency 1
Explore possible explanations for important evaluation findings.

Activity: School Health Education Program Evaluation

Student Outcome: The student can obtain a copy of a major comprehensive school health evaluation tool.

Directions:

1.   Obtain a copy of either the Healthy Schools 2000 checklist evaluation or the Criteria for Comprehensive Health Education Curricula (information for procuring both are found in the "Getting Started" section).

2.   Practice writing a cover letter to a school superintendent. Make up a hypothetical name or use the name of an administrator in your home town school district. In the letter explain what the evaluation tool is and why it is important to administer it in a school system.

3.   Attach the letter to the copy of the evaluation obtained in step one.

Getting Started

To obtain a copy of "Criteria for Comprehensive Health Education Curricula," contact: The Southwest Regional Educational Laboratory, 4665 Lampson Ave., Los Alamitos, CA 90720; (213) 598-7661.

For Healthy Schools 2000, contact: American School Health Association, PO Box 708, Kent, OH 44240; (216) 678-1601.

Evaluating Effectiveness of Health Education Programs

Competency D
Infer implications from findings for future program planning.

Sub-Competency 2
Recommend strategies for implementing results of evaluation.

Activity: Executive Summary

Student Outcome: The student can offer recommendations for implementing changes in a program based upon the results of the evaluation.

Directions:

1.   Find an article from a professional journal that describes the "evaluation" of a program, project, or activity.

2.   Using the following *executive summary* outline, write a one page summary of the journal article. Pay particular attention to the author's recommendations. If no recommendations are given, suggest at least two changes you would make in the program as a result of the evaluation data.

EXECUTIVE SUMMARY OUTLINE

* Background: purpose of program/project/activity
* Description: what was evaluated
* Purpose of Evaluation: why was it evaluated
* Methodology: how was the evaluation conducted; what instruments were used
* Results of the evaluation: what were the findings

Evaluating Effectiveness of Health Education Programs

Competency D
Infer implications from findings for future program planning.

Sub-Competency 2
Recommend strategies for implementing results of evaluations.

Activity: Objectives, Activities, Evaluation: Understanding The Relationships

Student Outcome: The student can explain how program objectives, learning activities, and program evaluation are interrelated.

Directions:

1.   Read the following section on the use of evaluation findings.

   Program Revision
   If your program is continuing or you have an opportunity to advise others who may plan similar programs, take time to apply what you have learned. For example:

   a. Reassess goals and objectives
       * Has anything changed (e.g., with the target audience, the community, or your
         agency's mission) to require revisions in the original goals and objectives?
       * Is there new information about the health issue that should be incorporated into
         the program messages or design?

   b. Determine areas where additional effort is needed
       * Are there objectives that are not being met? Why?
       * Are there strategies or activities that did not succeed? (Why didn't they work and
         what can be done to correct any problems?)
       * Are more resources required?

   c. Identify effective activities or strategies
       * Have some objectives been met as a result of existing activities?
       * Should these activities be continued without modification?
       * Should they be considered successful?
       * Can they be considered for use with other audiences or situations?

   d. Compare costs and results of different activities
       * What were the relative costs (including staff time) and results of different aspects
         of your program?
       * Are there some activities that indicate success, but cost less than others?

e. Reaffirm support for the program
  * Have you shared the results of your activities with the leadership of your agency?
  * Did you remember to share this information with the individuals and organizations outside your agency who contributed?
  * Do you have evidence of program effectiveness?
  * Do you have evidence of continued need to cite in convincing your agency to continue your program?
  * Do you have new or continuing activities that suggest the involvement of additional organizations?

f. Determine to end a program that did not work.

2. After reading, develop a one page summary explaining the interrelationships among objectives, learning activities, and evaluation strategies.

Getting Started

Material reprinted from:

National Cancer Institute. (1992). Making health communication programs work: A planner's guide. (NIH Publication No. 92-1493/t068). Bethesda, MD: Author.

Notes

Glossary of Terms

bipolar: a type of question used to measure attitudes with responses identified along a continuum, usually ranging from "strongly agree" to "strongly disagree"

chi square: statistical procedure that compares the differences in what is expected in the frequencies of different groups being compared and what is actually obtained

comparison group: a group of individuals not randomly assigned to an experimental or control group

executive summary: an overview of an evaluation that highlights why the study was conducted, how it was conducted, major results, and recommendations

experimental group: the group of individuals actually participating in the program

impact evaluation: assessment of the effects of the program interventions on the knowledge, skills, attitudes, and behaviors of the participants

intercept interviews: random survey of participants as they exit the program to assess satisfaction with the program

outcome evaluation: assessment of the effects of the program on the improvements in health and social factors

pilot test: pretesting a questionnaire, method, or materials on a small group prior to large scale administration

process evaluation: assessing the activities associated with the implementation of the program

qualitative methods: collecting information through interviews, observations, focus groups, or case studies to produce descriptions or soft data

quantitative methods: collecting information in the form of hard data, such as scores, ratings, counts, or classifications

reliability: the consistency and dependability of a measure

validity: the degree to which a test or instrument measures what it is supposed to measure

Notes

References

Dignan, M. B., & Carr, P. A. (1992). <u>Program planning for health education and promotion.</u> Philadelphia: Lea and Febiger.

Green, L. W., & Krueter, M. N. (1991). <u>Health promotion and planning: An educational and environmental approach.</u> Palo Alto, CA: Mayfield.

McKenzie, J. F., & Smeltzer, J. L. (1997). <u>Planning, implementing, and evaluating health promotion programs: A primer</u> (2nd ed.). Boston: Allyn and Bacon.

Muraskin, L. (1993). <u>Understanding evaluation: The way to better prevention programs.</u> Washington, DC: U.S. Department of Education.

National Cancer Institute. (1992). <u>Making health communications work: A planner's guide.</u> (NIH Publication No. 92-1493/t068). Bethesda, MD: Author.

Pirie, P. (1990). Evaluating Health Promotion Programs, in Bracht, N. (Ed.) <u>Health promotion at the community level.</u> Newbury Park, CA: Sage.

Simons-Morton, B., Greene, W., & Gottlieb, N. (1995). <u>Introduction to health education and health promotion.</u> Prospect Heights, IL: Waveland.

Timmreck, T. C. (1995). <u>Planning, program development, and evaluation: A handbook for health promotion, aging, and health services.</u> Boston: Jones and Bartlett.

Notes

5   *Coordinating Provision of Health Education Services*

A *health education coordinator* "is a professional health educator who is responsible for the management and coordination of all health education policies, activities, and resources within a particular setting or circumstance" (Joint Committee on Health Education Terminology, 1991, p. 180). The process of *coordination* involves "the orderly arrangement of group effort to provide unity of action in the pursuit of a common purpose" (Bedworth & Bedworth, 1992, p. 440).

The health education coordinator must know what agencies, organizations, individuals, and services are available to meet program needs and identify any overlapping services and/or gaps in services that may exist. People skills are necessary as the coordinator must bring individuals together, foster ownership, promote cooperation, and solicit feedback from all who are involved. In addition, the coordinator may become a conflict mediator when the need to defuse turf issues arises (Bedworth & Bedworth, 1992; National Commission for Health Education Credentialing, Inc., 1996; Simons-Morton, Greene, & Gottlieb, 1995).

One means of coordinating activities is coalition building. A *coalition* is "a temporary union of two or more individuals and/or organizations to achieve a common purpose" (McKenzie & Smeltzer, 1997, p. 164). Pooling resources and expertise of several groups in a collaborative effort can enhance the effectiveness of a health education program.

Another coordinating activity in which health educators engage is *in-service education*. Teachers in schools as well as health educators and volunteers in agencies and organizations need periodic in-service education. The purpose of in-service education programs is usually to update participants on content and/or demonstrate methods for meeting objectives and accomplishing program goals (Bedworth & Bedworth, 1992). In the remaining paragraphs, examples are provided to illustrate the health educator's role in the coordinating provision of health education services.

Community Health Setting

The health educator of the local chapter of the American Cancer Society is coordinating the Great American Smoke Out for the community. Information to the public is the primary focus of the educational campaign to encourage current smokers to quit. Well in advance of the Smoke Out date, the coordinator contacts other community organizations and individuals (e.g., local health department, respiratory therapy unit of the hospital, local physicians) for human resources and expertise to conduct various educational programs. In addition, the coordinator contacts the media (print and electronic) to advertise the Great American Smoke Out and special programs to be offered to the community, schools, and worksites. The coordinator, in cooperation with other organizations and institutions, schedules preventive programs, stop smoking clinics, and arranges the set up of educational/informational displays with the local library, civic center, and mall.

Medical Setting

The patient educator at the local hospital is collaborating with medical personnel and community health professionals to offer diabetes programming. These educational efforts are coordinated with direct medical care and treatment in an effort to increase understanding of treatment and compliance. The educator contacts the American Diabetes Association for educational/informational pamphlets and materials. In addition to contributing support materials for direct patient education during patient care, the educator offers a workshop on diabetes at the hospital for newly diagnosed diabetics and their families.

Post-Secondary Setting

The service committee of an *Eta Sigma Gamma* chapter is coordinating activities for World AIDS Day. They decide their focus will be a day-long series of educational events and programs. To plan and organize for these events, they create the "World AIDS Day Task Force," which is a coalition consisting of a peer educator from the Campus Wellness Program, a representative from American Red Cross, the AIDS educator from the local health department, the health educator at the University Health Service, and representatives from the school newspaper, and human service clubs, such as the Social Work Club or Family and Consumer Science Club. By bringing these people together for a common purpose, the process of coordinating programs begins.

School Setting

The administration of a school district has approved development and implementation of a comprehensive health education program in their schools. They have asked a middle school health educator to assume the role of coordinator of the project. The coordinator's first step is to recruit representatives from each of the following areas to be on the comprehensive health education committee: health services (school nurse), environment (custodian), worksite health promotion (faculty fitness club advocate), health instruction (health education teacher), school counseling and psychology (psychologist or counselor), food service (school dietician), and physical education (physical education teacher). In addition, a student, a parent (School Board member), and an administrator are invited to sit in on the curriculum committee.

Worksite Setting

To positively impact the health of employees, the company's health educator coordinates periodic meetings with personnel from other areas to discuss health needs of workers and to fill existing gaps. Currently, it is agreed that the Occupational Safety and Health Program will focus on employee safety training and programming, while the Employee Assistance Program will include mental health as well as drug and alcohol related programs. The medical staff will offer preventive health programming in the form of screening, while the Health Promotion Department will include stress management training, fitness and nutrition planning, and smoking cessation clinics.

Coordinating Provision of Health Education Services

Competency A
Develop a plan for coordinating health education services.

Sub-Competency 1
Determine the extent of available health education services.

Activity: Compiling A Resource Inventory

Student Outcome: The student can identify organizations in the community that may be used in compiling a community resource inventory for health promotion planning.

Directions:

1.   Listed below are general categories* of organizations that could be contacted to begin developing a resource inventory. Brainstorm a list of organizations, agencies, or individuals that are potential contacts for obtaining information about health programs or services. See the Business & Industry category for examples.

       Business & Industry: major worksites, restaurants, business coalitions, labor organizations, Chambers of Commerce, trade groups

       Community:

       Education:

       Health & Welfare:

       Information:

       Political & Legal:

       Recreation:

2. Select a community with which you are familiar. Using the same outline or categories, provide specific examples of contacts from your selected community. See the following example.

Business & Industry: State Farm Insurance, McDonald's, Bloomington Convention & Visitor's Bureau, United Auto Workers of America

Community:

Education:

Health & Welfare:

Information:

Political & Legal:

Recreation:

Getting Started

* Categories were adapted from:

Altman, D. (1989). Conducting a community resource inventory for health promotion planning. Palo Alto, CA: Stanford University School of Medicine.

For more information on a series of guides for health promotion planning, contact:

How-To Guides on Community Health
Health Promotion Resource Center
Stanford Center for Research in Disease Prevention
Stanford University School of Medicine
1000 Welch Road
Palo Alto, CA 94304-1885
(415) 723-1000

Coordinating Provision of Health Education Services

Competency A
Develop a plan for coordinating health education services.

Sub-Competency 1
Determine the extent of available health education services.

Activity: Health Education Services Search

Student Outcome: The student can explain how to locate health education services and identify available services in a chosen city.

Directions:

1.   A new public health department has been established in your county. As the new director of health education, your first task is to determine the extent of available health education services in the city.

2.   Explain the steps involved in locating available services.

3.   Choose a city with which you are familiar. Identify sites which provide health education services. List those available services.

4.   Describe any problems you encountered in identifying services in your chosen city.

5.   Develop a written report on your process and findings.

Coordinating Provision of Health Education Services

Competency A
Develop a plan for coordinating health education services.

Sub-Competency 2
Match health education services to proposed program activities.

Activity: Community Resource Checklist

Student Outcome: The student can match available health education services with program objectives.

Directions:

1.   Read the following scenario:

        A community recently experienced a series of emergencies and accidental deaths involving the misuse of inhalants by teenagers and preteens. You have been asked to assist with coordinating a prevention and treatment program to address the problem. Information listed in the Community Health Resource Directory indicates that several agencies already have services that could meet some of your objectives.

2.   Design a form or chart that could be used to help organize the information you gather concerning services in the community that might meet your program needs. Consider carefully what information needs to be gathered about each agency. For example, information such as who the contact person is for that agency, what the hours of operation are, and what services are offered might be considered.

3.   Title your document "Community Resource Guide."

Coordinating Provision of Health Education Services

Competency A
Develop a plan for coordinating health education services.

Sub-Competency 2
Match health education services to proposed program activities.

<u>Activity: Criteria For Correlation</u>

Student Outcome: The student can identify criteria for selecting health education agencies to match program activities.

Directions:

1.   Develop a list of possible "Earth Day" activities for your community.

2.   List health education agencies in your community that might contribute to the program activities you have identified. Place this list to the right of your activities list.

3.   Consider what criteria you, as the coordinator of "Earth Day," would use to match agencies with specific activities.

4.   Using the stated criteria, match agencies with "Earth Day" activities.
      Justify the match by identifying the criterion or criteria used.

Coordinating Provision of Health Education Services

Competency A
Develop a plan for coordinating health education services.

Sub-Competency 3
Identify gaps and overlaps in the provision of collaborative health services.

Activity: Drowning Prevention Plan

Student Outcome: The student can identify different health education services that have the potential to overlap.

Directions:

1.   Consider the following scenario:

        A university and community have become concerned with the number of accidental drownings among college students in a nearby lake. After the latest incident, there is increased talk about developing a safety education awareness program to address the problem. Numerous agencies, organizations, groups, and individuals have been quoted in the media as expressing an interest in developing a program. The various groups and agencies include:

        City Fire Department   University Safety Program
        City Recreation Department   University Health Promotion Center
        Local Public Health Department   University Athletic Department
        American Red Cross   Community Hospital Health Education Dept
        American Heart Association   A local church

2.   As a health educator, you recognize the need for coordinating efforts and services and the potential problems resulting from the lack of a coordination plan. On a separate sheet of paper, identify and describe the possible areas of overlap and duplication of services that could arise from the uncoordinated efforts of the agencies listed above. Be sure to make specific references to the agencies identified in the above scenario.

3.   If you were put in charge of developing the plan for coordinating a water safety and awareness program, describe how you would best utilize the agencies listed above in achieving the common goal: reducing the number of drownings at the lake.

Coordinating Provision of Health Education Services

Competency A
Develop a plan for coordinating health education services.

Sub-Competency 3
Identify gaps and overlaps in the provision of collaborative health services.

Activity: Gap And Overlap

Student Outcome: The student can identify gaps and overlaps of health education services among selected health agencies.

Directions:

1.   Obtain an annual report from three different types of health agencies or organizations in your area. Examples of appropriate agencies or organizations include: public health department, hospital, mental health center, or voluntary health organizations focusing on cardiovascular health, cancer, lung disease, etc.

2.   Using a sheet of paper divided into three sections, identify the services provided by each agency.

3.   Identify gaps and overlaps in health education services among the health agencies.

4.   Describe how these agencies/organizations can reduce these gaps and overlaps. What actions need to occur to address these concerns?

Coordinating Provision of Health Education Services

Competency B
Facilitate cooperation between and among levels of program personnel.

Sub-Competency 1
Promote cooperation and feedback among personnel related to the program.

<u>Activity:</u> <u>Assessing Meeting Effectiveness</u>

Student Outcome: The student can observe and evaluate the group meeting process.

Directions:

1.   Attend and observe a group meeting. This can be any type of meeting, such as a community group, a committee, an administration meeting, a student group, etc.

2.   Use the "Assessing Meeting Effectiveness" form provided to record your observations.

ASSESSING MEETING EFFECTIVENESS

Name of Group: _____ **Date:** _____

Number in Attendance: _____ **Meeting Length:** _____

		Yes	No
1.	A facilitator was present	____	____
2.	A record keeper was assigned or identified	____	____
3.	An agenda was available	____	____
4.	The meeting started on time	____	____
5.	The meeting ended on time	____	____

		Strongly Disagree	Disagree	Undecided	Agree	Strongly Agree
6.	The facilitator was effective in keeping the group on task	1	2	3	4	5
7.	Members of the group appeared interested and attentive	1	2	3	4	5
8.	All group members contributed to the discussion	1	2	3	4	5
9.	The meeting was organized	1	2	3	4	5
10.	The meeting was purposeful	1	2	3	4	5

11.   What were strengths of the facilitator?

12.   What were weaknesses of the facilitator?

Other observations:

Notes

Coordinating Provision of Health Education Services

Competency B
Facilitate cooperation between and among levels of program personnel.

Sub-Competency 1
Promote cooperation and feedback among personnel related to the program.

Activity: Promoting Cooperation

Student Outcome: The student can identify ways to obtain feedback and encourage cooperation in situations where there is conflict among personnel in a program.

Directions:

1.   Select one of the two scenarios described below, depending on your interest in a school or community-based setting.

School: You are coordinating the high school health education program in which there are both full-time and part-time health teachers. One task you are coordinating is selection of a new health textbook for the next school year. During this process, several teachers confide to you that their opinions are not valued because they only teach health part-time.

Community: While employed as a health educator in a public health department, you are able to buy a new "top-of-the-line" computer through grant money. There are four health educators who will be using the new computer. Conflict among personnel is developing regarding where the computer will be located and how priority will be established for using it.

2.   Develop a memo in which you address the following issues:

a. Identify the problem.
b. Ask for feedback in resolving the problem.
c. Identify the mechanism for obtaining program feedback (perhaps a group meeting or everyone sending their ideas by e-mail).
d. Conclude by encouraging a spirit of cooperation among program personnel.

Getting Started

Many word processing software packages have a template selection. You may want to use the "memo" template for this activity.

Coordinating Provision of Health Education Services

Competency B
Facilitate cooperation between and among levels of program personnel.

Sub-Competency 2
Apply various methods of conflict reduction as needed.

Activity: Conflict Reduction

Student Outcome: The student can distinguish between various methods of conflict reduction by providing examples of each.

Directions:

1.   Discuss with others meanings for the terms "mediation," "arbitration," and "negotiation." After reaching group consensus, complete the chart below with definitions for the conflict reduction terms listed:

Mediation:
Arbitration:
Negotiation:

2.   Using the worksheet on the following page, describe realistic scenarios involving situations or settings in which a health educator may be in the position to "mediate," "arbitrate," and "negotiate" (one scenario for each term). Try to create scenarios involving the various settings in which health educators work (i.e., community, medical, post-secondary, school, or worksite).

CONFLICT REDUCTION

Scenario #1 - Mediation

Scenario #2 - Arbitration

Scenario #3 - Negotiation

Notes

Coordinating Provision of Health Education Services

Competency B
Facilitate cooperation between and among levels of program personnel.

Sub-Competency 2
Apply various methods of conflict reduction as needed.

<u>Activity:</u> <u>Utilizing Communication Techniques In Resolving Conflicts</u>

Student Outcome: The student can identify effective and poor verbal and non-verbal communication techniques that can either assist or hinder resolution of conflict.

Directions:

1.   Within the class, divide into groups of four. If there is an uneven number, some groups can have five members, with the fifth member explaining the scenario to others.

2.   In this activity, each group will be role-playing effective and poor verbal and non-verbal communication.

3.   In your group, divide into pairs. Pair A should decide on two examples of poor verbal communication and two examples of poor non-verbal communication. For example, the pair might select "interrupting" for poor verbal and "arms folded across the chest" for poor nonverbal. Pair B should do the same, but decide on two examples of both effective verbal and non-verbal communication techniques.

4.   Decide on a situation involving conflict. Perhaps you might select the school setting in which two teachers are in conflict over how to handle a problem with a student. In the community setting, two health educators might be in conflict over the date and location of an educational program.

5.   In front of the class, first explain the situation and the conflict. Pair A goes first and completes the role play, demonstrating the poor communication techniques. Pair B then does the same role play, but demonstrates good communication techniques.

6.   After the role play, ask other class members to identify the effective and poor communication techniques that were demonstrated. Write those on the board.

7.   Each group will complete their role play in front of the class and the techniques generated will be written on the board.

Coordinating Provision of Health Education Services

Competency B
Facilitate cooperation between and among levels of program personnel.

Sub-Competency 3
Analyze the role of health educator as liaison between program staff and outside groups and organizations.

<u>Activity: Establishing An Advisory Council</u>

Student Outcome: The student can identify potential advisory council members from outside community organizations and serve as a liaison between these potential members and program staff by coordinating the initial meeting.

Directions:

1.   Select one of the two following scenarios, depending on your area of interest:

    a. You are a school health educator in a school system that has five other health educators on staff. You want to adopt and implement a new high school health education curriculum that includes increased coverage of human sexuality issues. To facilitate implementation, your principal asks you to establish an Advisory Council.

    b. You are a health educator in a public health department that has received a grant to implement a community-based program to stop underage drinking and driving. As part of the grant, you need to establish an Advisory Council.

2.   Identify a list of ten persons, representing different interests, whom you would ask to serve (for example, parents, police, religious leaders).

3.   Write a business letter that could be sent to each potential member. Include in the letter the following information:

    a. An explanation of your involvement in the project.
    b. Purpose of the Advisory Council.
    c. Obligation for those individuals who accept (meetings per year, length of meetings, etc.).
    d. The first meeting date, time, and location.
    e. Procedure for individual to follow in accepting or refusing membership on Advisory Council (for example, a phone call, response postcard, etc.).

4.   Consider the first Advisory Council meeting and your role as liaison between staff and Advisory Council members:

    a. If you need to conduct the first meeting, what planning should be done in advance? (i.e., sending confirmation letters, developing name tags)

    b. During the first minutes, how would you start the meeting? How would introductions be made? What type of information about each Advisory Council member and his/her agency would you want to collect?

    c. On a separate sheet of paper, prepare a list of ideas for answering questions in 4a. Then describe how you would start the meeting, make introductions, etc., for 4b. Attach this sheet to the business letter for submission to the instructor.

Getting Started

For a reference on writing business letters, refer to:

    Dugger, J. (1996). Business letters for busy people (3rd ed.). Shawnee Mission, KS: National Press.

Coordinating Provision of Health Education Services

Competency B
Facilitate cooperation between and among levels of program personnel.

Sub-Competency 3
Analyze the role of health educator as liaison between program staff and outside groups and organizations.

<u>Activity: Writing A Job Description</u>

Student Outcome: The student can demonstrate how to write an appropriate job description for a health education job.

Directions:

1.   You are the coordinator for a hospital-based health promotion program. You need to hire an instructor to teach the upcoming first aid and safety component of the program. As liaison for your program and hospital staff, you must prepare a job description to communicate the need for an instructor. Consider some of the questions listed below in preparation for writing your job description for the position:

   * What are the goals/objectives of this component of the program?
   * How does this job fit into the program as a whole?
   * What will be the responsibilities of the person hired for this position?
   * What qualifications will the person hired need to have to achieve the program goals/objectives?

2.   On a separate sheet of paper, write the job description using these descriptors: job title, responsibilities, qualifications, salary range, and application procedures.

<u>Getting Started</u>

You can find some examples of job descriptions in many professional journals, college or university placement centers, the *HEDIR*, or in your local newspaper's Help Wanted section.

Coordinating Provision of Health Education Services

Competency C
Formulate practical modes of collaboration among health agencies and organizations.

Sub-Competency 1
Stimulate development of cooperation among personnel responsible for community health education programs.

Activity: Interview With A Health Coordinator

Student Outcome: The student can describe situations in which *collaboration* among health personnel and agencies/organizations occurs, offer suggestions as to how to facilitate cooperation, and list strategies for circumventing roadblocks that may occur.

Directions:

1.   Contact a health educator in one of the five major settings (community health, medical, post-secondary, school, or worksite) to schedule a 30 minute interview.

2.   Use the interview form on the following page as a guide. Add two to three questions of your own.

3.   It might be helpful to send the interviewee a copy of the interview guide a few days before the interview.

4.   Within two to three days after the interview, send a thank you note to the interviewee.

Notes

INTERVIEW WITH A HEALTH COORDINATOR

_____   _____
(Name of Interviewee)   (Job Title)

Job Responsibilities:

_____

_____

Educational Background/Training: _____

_____

Interview Questions: (Interviewer may wish to tape and/or take notes)

1.   Can you describe several specific situations in which you have facilitated or
        encouraged cooperation among personnel responsible for a program?

2.   What strategies have you used to foster cooperation among individuals and/or
        groups?

3.   What specific skills are needed to facilitate cooperation?

4.   What are the most common roadblocks to cooperation that you have experienced?

5.   What suggestions can you make for avoiding potential roadblocks?

6.   What recommendations can you give me to prepare myself for coordinating
        collaborative efforts among individuals, agencies, and/or organizations? (skills,
        courses, etc.)

Notes

Coordinating Provision of Health Education Services

Competency C
Formulate practical modes of collaboration among health agencies and organizations.

Sub-Competency 1
Stimulate development of cooperation among personnel responsible for community health education programs.

Activity: Tips To Success In Communication

Student Outcome: The student can identify factors which contribute to successful communication and positive interpersonal relationships.

Directions:

1.   Open communication and positive interpersonal relationships are important components of a successful program. In the left column of the worksheets provided, identify "tips to success" for open communication and positive interpersonal relationships. Answering the following questions may help trigger responses for the worksheet.

        * What communication factors have helped you to understand someone or something?
        * What factors have contributed to a positive interpersonal relationship in your life?

2.   On the right side of each worksheet, identify "barriers to success" for open communication and positive interpersonal relationships. Answering the following questions may help trigger responses for the worksheet.

        * What actions or factors have caused communication to cease?
        * What actions or factors have caused an interpersonal relationship to deteriorate?

3.   In the space below, describe why open communication and positive interpersonal relationships are important to the success of a program or agency.

Notes

TIPS TO SUCCESS IN COMMUNICATION:
OPEN COMMUNICATION

Tips for Success	Barriers to Success

TIPS TO SUCCESS IN COMMUNICATION: POSITIVE INTERPERSONAL RELATIONSHIPS

Tips for Success	Barriers to Success

Coordinating Provision of Health Education Services

Competency C
Formulate practical modes of collaboration among health agencies and organizations.

Sub-Competency 2
Suggest approaches for integrating health education within existing health programs.

Activity: Integrating Health Education

Student Outcome: The student can describe how existing health programs might integrate a *health observance*.

Directions:

1.   Select a health observance not usually observed on your campus or in your community (refer to the ASHA Network News listing of health observances or a similar list).

2.   Within one setting (i.e., community health, medical, post-secondary, school, or worksite), make a list of all existing health programs of which you are aware by using the worksheet that follows.

3.   Explain how the health observance topic you have chosen can be integrated into one or more of the existing programs.

Getting Started

For example, National Minority Cancer Awareness Week occurs in April. Although your college has several health programs in place (Wellness Center, Student Health Service, Health Advocates, etc.), minority cancer awareness has not been a focus of any of these programs in recent years. The Wellness Center might offer educational programs on campus to increase the awareness of cancer incidence and prevalence in minority groups. The Student Health Services might contact the Office of Minority Health Resource Center for informational pamphlets and brochures on cancer in minorities to have available in the waiting room. Health Advocates may wish to target African American fraternities and sororities with an informational program about cancer prevention.

Notes

INTEGRATING HEALTH EDUCATION

_____
(Health Observance)

Selected Setting: _____

Agencies/Groups/Organizations

How the health observance topic can be integrated

1.

2.

3.

4.

5.

Notes

Coordinating Provision of Health Education Services

Competency C
Formulate practical modes of collaboration among health agencies and organizations.

Sub-Competency 2
Suggest approaches for integrating health education within existing health programs.

Activity: Does It Fit?

Student Outcome: The student can identify how to integrate health education into other existing programs.

Directions:

1.   As a health education consultant, you have contracted with three organizations or institutions to determine the best way to integrate health education into existing programs. The organizations or institutions include a hospital, an industry, and a senior citizen community center. None of these facilities has a current health education component.

2.   Identify a specific hospital, industry, and senior citizen community center in your area.

3.   Using the worksheet on the following page, identify programs currently being offered at these sites.

4.   Determine where various health education programs on topics such as nutrition/diet, safety, smoking cessation, cardiovascular health, or exercise can be integrated into the existing programs. For example, an industry has an employee assistance program (EAP) currently in place. A stress management program may be incorporated into this EAP structure utilizing the EAP counselor already on site. Share your findings with others.

Notes

DOES IT FIT?

Hospital	Industry	Senior Citizen Community Center
Name:	Name:	Name:

Notes

Coordinating Provision of Health Education Services

Competency C
Formulate practical modes of collaboration among health agencies and organizations.

Sub-Competency 3
Develop plans for promoting collaborative efforts among health agencies and organizations with mutual interests.

Activity: A Master Plan

Student Outcome: The student can develop a master plan to promote a special health observance among campus health agencies and organizations.

Directions:

1.   Identify three health agencies and/or organizations that advocate comprehensive school health education programs (e.g., American School Health Association, American Cancer Society, Division of Adolescent and School Health of the Centers for Disease Control and Prevention, American Association for Health Education, state level school health organization).

2.   Request a copy of each agency's mission statement, as well as information on the purposes, goals, and objectives of their programs on comprehensive school health education.

3.   Compare and contrast similarities and differences among the materials received. How are the mission statements similar and/or different? How is comprehensive school health education defined? What are the components of comprehensive school health education? How do the agencies advocate implementing comprehensive school health education?

4.   Identify the common ground in mission statements as well as the comprehensive school health education program goals and objectives.

5.   Analyze, in a written paper, how this information can be useful in encouraging collaborative efforts among the agencies you have selected.

Coordinating Provision of Health Education Services

Competency C
Formulate practical modes of collaboration among health agencies and organizations.

Sub-Competency 3
Develop plans for promoting collaborative efforts among health agencies and organizations with mutual interests.

<u>Activity: Defining Collaboration</u>

Student Outcome: The student can define collaboration and explain functions involved in effective collaboration.

Directions:

1.   Define collaboration in your own words using the space below.

2.   Explain the function of collaboration in health education. Provide a specific example to demonstrate your understanding of the term collaboration between individuals or among groups and agencies.

3.   Describe how individuals, groups, or agencies can initiate collaborative efforts.

4.   Describe how to maintain collaborative efforts once they have been successfully initiated.

Coordinating Provision of Health Education Services

Competency D
Organize in-service training for teachers, volunteers, and other interested personnel.

Sub-Competency 1
Plan an operational, competency oriented training program.

Activity: Community In-Service Education

Student Outcome: The student can develop objectives and an agenda for *in-service education (ISE)* based on a community need.

Directions:

1.   You are a health educator with the American Red Cross in a large community with numerous social service and health-related agencies. During the past year, there have been several cases of Hepatitis B reported.

2.   You have been asked to provide a three hour in-service education program for service providers in your community concerning Hepatitis B and other blood-borne pathogens. Universal Precautions must also be addressed.

3.   The in-service program has been scheduled for a Friday morning from 9:00 am - noon. Approximately 50 people will be in attendance.

4.   Using the form on the following page as a guide, plan this in-service education program. You may want to check resources on Hepatitis B to help in planning.

Getting Started

American Red Cross. (March 1993). Preventing disease transmission. St. Louis, MO: Mosby Lifeline.

Notes

COMMUNITY IN-SERVICE EDUCATION

Title of In-Service Program: _____

Date, Time, Location: _____

At least five learner objectives:

1.

2.

3.

4.

5.

Training Agenda

Account for all three hours of time (for example, 9:00 - 9:15 for the introduction, 9:15 - 10:00 for overview of blood-borne pathogens, etc.). Include time for introductions, break(s), and evaluation. What are the main topic areas that should be addressed? In what order?

Notes

Coordinating Provision of Health Education Services

Competency D
Organize in-service training for teachers, volunteers, and other interested personnel.

Sub-Competency 1
Plan an operational, competency oriented training program.

Activity: In-Service Education And Adult Learning Principles

Student Outcome: The student can plan in-service education based on principles of adult learning.

Directions:

1.   Review information on adult learning principles discussed in the works of M. S. Knowles, A. B. Knox, F. H. Wood and S. R. Thompson, and S. N. Orlich.

2.   Based on the understanding of these principles, discuss how each principle could affect organizing and delivering two half-day in-service programs provided by the school district for junior and senior high school health education teachers. The topic for the in-service program is conflict resolution as determined by earlier teacher input for topics to be addressed during the institute or in-service days.

3.   Share your ideas with others on the importance and value of adult learning principles as guides for consideration when organizing in-service education programs.

Getting Started

Recommended readings:

Knowles, M. S. (1980). The modern practice of adult education (rev. ed.). Chicago: Association/Follet Press.

Knowles, M. S. (1984). The adult learner: A neglected species (3rd ed.). Houston: Gulf Publishing.

Knox, A. B. (1978). Adult development and learning. San Francisco: Jossey-Bass.

Orlich, D. C. (1989). Staff development: Enhancing human potential. Boston: Allyn and Bacon.

Wood, F. H., & Thompson, S. R. (1980). Guidelines for better staff development. Educational Leadership, 37, 374-378.

Think of the following five aspects of organizing an in-service program and to what degree, if any, each of the adult learning principles should be applied.

* identifying learner needs for information and skill building
* planning measurable in-service program objectives
* selecting learning activities to achieve stated learner needs
* determining criteria for selection of qualified in-service education personnel
* describing the role of the learner and role of the leader before, during, and after the in-service program

Coordinating Provision of Health Education Services

Competency D
Organize in-service training for teachers, volunteers, and other interested personnel.

Sub-Competency 2
Utilize instructional resources that meet a variety of in-service training needs.

<u>Activity: Instructional Resources A La Carte</u>

Student Outcome: The student can produce a packet of instructional resources for use in an in-service education (ISE) program designed for volunteers.

Directions:

1.   Choose a topic area for training adult volunteers in a two hour in-service program preparing volunteers to deliver health education programs in the school or community. For example, the topic may be heart health, with volunteers being trained to deliver two short lessons to elementary-age students on maintaining a healthy heart.

2.   Due to time constraints and the range of topics to be covered, you decide as the in-service education program planner to provide each participant with an instructional resources packet. The purpose of the packet is to provide volunteers with additional take-home resources to enhance their readiness to implement the program, and to aid them in accessing additional information, if desired.

3.   Put together a packet of materials for the volunteers, including both resources on the chosen topic and the characteristics of the target audience. Consider different types of resources as suggested in the following list:

* brochure on topic
* fact sheet on topic or agency sponsoring in-service education program
* magazine article with appropriate reading level for volunteers
* toll-free numbers relevant to topic
* chart describing interests, needs, behaviors of target audience
* Internet addresses appropriate to the content topic or growth and development characteristics of target audience

4.   Remember, the packet of additional resources supplements the program materials provided to the volunteers for actual use in program delivery to the audience (i.e., a video used as a trigger, models, posters, handouts, and lesson plans).

Coordinating Provision of Health Education Services

Competency D
Organize in-service training for teachers, volunteers, and other interested personnel.

Sub-Competency 2
Utilize instructional resources that meet a variety of in-service training needs.

Activity: Instructional Resources: How Do You Choose?

Student Outcome: The student can establish and justify selection of instructional resources by developing criteria to appraise the applicability of those resources.

Directions:

1.   Within the state where you are working, the governor has provided grants to local public health departments to provide programs to reduce the incidence of teenage pregnancies.

2.   At a statewide conference on public health issues, you have been asked to provide a two-hour in-service program to public health educators who have received grant money. A large number of participants, with a variety of backgrounds and experiences in working with the issue of teenage pregnancies, is expected to attend.

3.   A number of training videos and brochures are available, but you have enough money to purchase only one video and one set of brochures for your training.

4.   During class time, divide into small groups. Using the following worksheet, formulate at least three criteria your group will use to assess the best resource materials for the in-service education program. Briefly justify each of the criteria.

Getting Started

For a free copy of Making health communication programs work: A planner's guide (NIH Publication No. 92-1493/t068), call 1-800-4-CANCER, or write a letter of request to:

National Cancer Institute's Cancer Information Service
31 Center Drive MSC 2580
Building 31, Room 10A16
Bethesda, MD 20892-2580

INSTRUCTIONAL RESOURCES: HOW DO YOU CHOOSE?

In-Service Education for Teenage Pregnancy Reduction Grant Recipients

Brochure

Criterion 1:

Justification:

Criterion 2:

Justification:

Criterion 3:

Justification:

Video

Criterion 1:

Justification:

Criterion 2:

Justification:

Criterion 3:

Justification:

Notes

Coordinating Provision of Health Education Services

Competency D
Organize in-service training for teachers, volunteers, and other interested personnel.

Sub-Competency 3
Demonstrate a wide range of strategies for conducting in-service training programs.

Activity: Group Size And Strategies: What Is The Relationship?

Student Outcome: The student can identify how selection of instructional strategies may vary depending on size of group and training facility.

Directions:

1.   For this activity, select one of the two scenarios based upon your interests.

      a. You are a school health educator who was selected to be educated in a conflict resolution program for high school students. You are required to conduct in-service programs throughout the state.

      b. As a prevention specialist in a community-based organization, you received in-service education in "Inhalant Abuse in Adolescence." You are required to conduct in-service programs throughout the state.

2.   Imagine two possible in-service scenarios. In the first scenario, you will be conducting an education session with over 100 people in attendance located at a university auditorium. In the second scenario, you will be providing in-service education at smaller regional settings held in classrooms at local high schools. No more than 25 people will be in attendance at each training.

3.   On the following worksheet, answer the questions concerning instructional methods.

Notes

GROUPS SIZE AND STRATEGIES: WHAT IS THE RELATIONSHIP?

1.   What type of instructional strategies would be appropriate for use with the large group in an auditorium?

2.   Provide two examples of how selection of instructional strategies might change with the small groups in the classrooms.

3.   If you were to conduct these in-service programs, would you select the large or small group? Why?

4.   Do you feel that the learning process is affected by size of group? If yes, describe in what ways learning is affected.

Notes

Coordinating Provision of Health Education Services

Competency D
Organize in-service training for teachers, volunteers, and other interested personnel.

Sub-Competency 3
Demonstrate a wide range of strategies for conducting in-service training programs.

Activity: In-Service Strategies Exploration

Student Outcome: The student can compare and contrast instructional strategies of two models for in-service education in terms of learner success.

Directions:

1.   Read the following article to identify specific instructional strategies of two in-service education (ISE) models:

        Spark, D., & Loucks-Horsley, S. (1989). Five models of staff development.

        Journal of Staff Development, 10 (4), 40-57.

2.   List the instructional strategies of each model in the chart on the following page. Then provide reasons cited in the article for each selected ISE model strategy. Last, note any information, such as research studies, given on relationships of instructional method and learner success.

Notes

IN-SERVICE STRATEGIES EXPLORATION

Model Name:		
Instructional Strategy	Reasons for Inclusion	Impact on Learner Success

Model Name:		
Instructional Strategy	Reasons for Inclusion	Impact on Learner Success

Notes

Glossary of Terms

coalition: formation of a union of distinct parties or persons for the purpose of joint action toward a common goal

collaboration: the act of working together, especially toward an intellectual endeavor

coordination: the process of acting together toward a common purpose in a harmonious manner

Eta Sigma Gamma: the national professional health education honorary

health education coordinator: health educator whose responsibility it is to integrate all health education activities and resources in a particular setting or situation

health observance: recognition of a health-related event or occurrence, usually on a given date or during a given week or month

HEDIR (Health Education Directory): an electronic mail listserv technique for sending health education related memos to subscribers of that listserv; developed and copywrited by Mark J. Kittleson, Ph.D.

in-service education (ISE): planned programs based on identified needs and specific objectives to extend, add, or improve job-oriented knowledge, skills, or competencies of employees

Notes

References

Bedworth, A. E., & Bedworth, D. A. (1992). <u>The profession and practice of health education.</u> Dubuque, IA: Wm. C. Brown.

Joint Committee on Health Education Terminology. (1991). Report of the 1990 Joint Committee on Health Education Terminology. <u>Journal of Health Education, 22</u> (3), 173-184.

McKenzie, J. F., & Smeltzer, J. L. (1997). <u>Planning, implementing, and evaluating health promotion programs: A primer</u> (2nd ed.). Boston: Allyn and Bacon.

National Commission for Health Education Credentialing, Inc. (1996). <u>A competency-based framework for professional development of certified health education specialists.</u> Allentown, PA: Author.

Simons-Morton, B. G., Greene, W. H., & Gottlieb, N. H. (1995). <u>Introduction to health education and health promotion.</u> Prospect Heights, IL: Waveland.

Notes

6   *Acting as a Resource Person in Health Education*

The interest in health education and health information has increased as connections continue to be made among risk factors, personal behavior, health, and disease (Department of Health and Human Services, 1991). Health conscious individuals, consumers of health, and health professionals are seeking and requesting more information. In addition to many other responsibilities, the health educator must be an accessible, accurate, and responsible resource for health information. To be an effective resource person, the health educator needs to be technologically competent in utilizing computerized health information retrieval systems. Familiarity with on-line systems and databases, such as *MEDLINE*, *Educational Resources Information Center (ERIC)*, *Combined Health Information Database (CHID)*, *Medical and Psychological Previews*, and *PsycINFO* is essential.

Examples of other online databases that address specific topics include *Agricola* (human nutrition), *Sport Database* (sports medicine), and *Druginfo* (substance abuse). The health educator must also be acquainted with health information centers and clearinghouses, such as the *National Health Information Center (NHIC)*, *Center for Health Promotion and Education*, and *Clearinghouse on Health Indexes*. Many topic-specific clearinghouses are also available.

Acting as a resource person often places the health educator in a consulting role. Consulting involves an informed individual sharing his/her experience and knowledge with another person to assist with decision-making and problem-solving (Simons-Morton, Greene, & Gottlieb, 1995). As a health educator is called upon to provide assistance to those with technical or process needs, it is important to understand the skills and abilities required to provide that service. This includes identifying and understanding individual strengths and areas of expertise, as well as weaknesses and limitations in knowledge and experiences. The health educator needs to understand the nature and scope of health *consultation* and consulting requests, as well as identifying sites, facilities, and relationships appropriate for effective consultation (National Commission for Health Education Credentialing [NCHEC], Inc., 1996).

In addition to consulting, the health educator will be asked to respond to requests for health information and make appropriate referrals. The referral process will require the health educator to be able to interpret the information requests and use a variety of efficient and effective approaches to direct those with requests to appropriate sources of health information.

Being a resource person also will require the health educator to compare and evaluate the worth of educational resource materials such as print materials, audiovisual aid(s), and interactive media (NCHEC, 1996). Materials can be evaluated and categorized according to cost, target group, developmental level, and cultural sensitivity. Being familiar with resource materials and keeping up-to-date on what is available will enable the health educator to be an effective resource person. In the next few paragraphs, examples will be provided to illustrate the role of the health educator acting as a resource person in a variety of settings.

Community Health Setting

A community task force has been established to address the sale of tobacco products to underage children. The task force is attempting to convince the city council to prohibit the use of cigarette vending machines anywhere within the city limits. The health educator for the American Cancer Society is asked to be the health resource person for the task force. The committee needs valid, reliable, up-to-date information to convince the city council of the seriousness of the situation and to show the success of other cities using this approach. Using computerized health information retrieval systems, the health educator provides current statistics and data regarding the topic as well as descriptions of model programs other communities have used to address the problem.

Medical Setting

An HMO sets up a health information referral service available to its members through a toll free telephone number. A health educator is hired to coordinate the service. Since a wide variety of calls are anticipated, the coordinator hires operators and trains them to analyze each specific request for information. The operators will attempt to distinguish between the need for just health information or interest in health education programs. They also will be trained to respond formally or informally to the requests and to recognize health misconceptions held by the callers in order to better direct their requests.

Post-Secondary Setting

A Health Education Resource Center at a university is establishing a Peer Education Program. The center's health educator is responsible for ordering resource materials that will be used by the peer educators in their programs. A specific budget has been established for the materials and supplies. The health educator must select and order the appropriate resources to meet the needs and objectives of the various programs while working within budgetary constraints.

School Setting

A school health educator is involved with a committee at the state level in developing a new, comprehensive school health education curriculum. The committee's task now is to get the curriculum accepted and implemented by schools. The school health educator makes several suggestions to committee members concerning the most effective way to disseminate the materials. The committee decides to use three methods on a trial basis to allow them to compare and choose the most effective distribution method.

Worksite Setting

A local manufacturing company is in the proces of reorganizing for the future. Part of the new vision involves the establishment of a wellness program for its employees. A health educator is initially interviewed as a potential consultant to the company to develop a plan for implementing the program. The health educator suggests the company draw up a contract inclusive of the job description, responsibilities, and services that are desired. Both the health educator and company executives agree that the consultant will provide a written report outlining the details for conducting a needs assessment, developing goals and objectives, designing an implementation plan, developing the evaluation plan, and preparing a program budget. The report will be completed and presented to the company executives within a year of the contract signing.

Acting as a Resource Person in Health Education

Competency A
Utilize computerized health information retrieval system effectively.

Sub-Competency 1
Match an information need with the appropriate retrieval system.

Activity: Differences In Databases

Student Outcome: The student can identify types of computerized databases and the different types of information that each provides.

Directions:

1.   Use your campus library to complete this assignment. You might talk with a librarian, use information sheets that are provided in most libraries, and use the thesauri that accompany the computerized databases.

2.   Listed are a number of computerized databases available in most libraries. Select any three to use in this assignment. Examples include:

        * ERIC
        * GPO (Government Printing Office)
        * Infotrac
        * Medline
        * PsycLIT (Psychological Abstracts)
        * Reader's Guide Abstracts

3.   For each of the databases selected, identify where in the library each is located. What types of journals or other publications are indexed in each database? Write down your findings.

4.   After selecting a content area and target group group (violence and adolescents, senior citizens and medication use, for example), conduct a computerized search on each of the three databases. Print the abstracts, if allowed, for the first ten "hits" on each search.

5.   Discuss "hits" that are similar and different on the databases. Why is it important to match the health information need with the appropriate database?

Acting as a Resource Person in Health Education

Competency A
Utilize computerized health information retrieval system effectively.

Sub-Competency 1
Match an information need with the appropriate retrieval system.

Activity: Online Health-Related Database Identification

Student Outcome: The student can identify online health-related databases appropriate to specific health information needs.

Directions:

1.   Choose five health topics of interest. These topics may include specific content areas (e.g., sexuality, substance abuse, consumer health, etc.) or specific health problems/disorders.

2.   Identify three online health-related databases for each topic. Indicate whether a charge is necessary for the retrieval of information.

3.   List the steps taken to retrieve information and the online address for each database chosen.

Getting Started

The following URLs on the World Wide Web are helpful places to start your investigation:

http://cedr.lbl.gov/cdrom/lookup	(1990 Census Lookup)
http://wwwonder.cdc.gov/	(CDC Wonder)
http://nlm.nih.gov/	(National Library of Medicine Online Databases and Databanks)

Acting as a Resource Person in Health Education

Competency A
Utilize computerized health information retrieval system effectively.

Sub-Competency 2
Access principal on-line and other database health information resources.

Activity: Assessing The "Net"

Student Outcome: The student can utilize and assess Internet sites that can be used for health information.

Directions:

1. Select any topic of interest to you regarding health issues. Narrow the topic to a specific area. For example, select "eating disorders" rather than nutrition, or "lead poisoning" rather than environmental health.

2. Use a *search engine*, such as Yahoo or WebCrawler, on the Internet to identify possible sites. Feel free to "*link*" to other possible sites. Spend some time examining sites.

3. Select at least 10 sites related to your topic (avoid taking the first ten that appear in order). Print the "*home page*" for each. In addition, review the site and make notes on what information is available. For example, who maintains the site? Are any credientials listed? Does it link to other sites? When was the site last updated? Read the article listed under "Getting Started" if you need ideas on how to assess an Internet site.

4. Submit a paper with a one paragraph description for each site. Explain what is available on the site and assess the reliability of the site. Attach the "home pages" to this paper.

Getting Started

Larkin, M. (1996). Health information on-line. FDA Consumer, 30 (5), 21-25.

Acting as a Resource Person in Health Education

Competency A
Utilize computerized health information retrieval system effectively.

Sub-Competency 2
Access principal on-line and other database health information resources.

<u>Activity: Online Health-Related Database Information Retrieval</u>

Student Outcome: The student can access health information from online health-related databases.

Directions:

1.   Locate the information gathered in the activity "Online Health-Related Database Identification."

2.   For each topic chosen, identify a question to be answered (e.g., what is the incubation period for HIV?).

3.   From two databases, retrieve and briefly summarize in a few sentences the information obtained in answering each question.

4.   Provide the appropriate reference citation in American Psychological Association (APA) format for each source from which information was obtained.

<u>Getting Started</u>

Examples of APA style citations for electronic sources can be found at the following URL on the World Wide Web:

http://www.uvm.edu/~xli/reference/apa.html

Acting as a Resource Person in Health Education

Competency B
Establish effective consultive relationships with those requesting assistance in solving health-related problems.

Sub-Competency 1
Analyze parameters of effective consultative relationships.

<u>Activity:</u> <u>Defining The Boundaries Of Health Consultation</u>

Student Outcome: The student can describe the nature and scope of health consultation and differentiate between informal and formal consultation.

Directions:

1.   Describe the nature and scope of health consultation.

2.   Differentiate between informal and formal consultation.

3.   Consulting takes place in a variety of settings and through a variety of methods. Describe settings and methods utilized in informal and formal consultation.

Acting as a Resource Person in Health Education

Competency B
Establish effective consultative relationships with those requesting assistance in solving health-related problems.

Sub-Competency 1
Analyze parameters of effective consultative relationships.

<u>Activity</u>: <u>Developing Consultative Relationships</u>

Student Outcome: The student can describe the methods for developing consultative relationships.

Directions:

1.   Interview two health education/promotion professionals currently working in your community or a nearby community who have been involved in health consultation. These individuals may be employed at the local hospital, public health department, schools (K-12 or college levels), or voluntary health organization.

2.   According to Deeds, Cleary, and Neiger (1996), there are six phases of consultation (p. 65):

        * Contact and entry
        * Contract and establish relationship
        * Problem identification--analysis
        * Goal setting and planning
        * Taking action and cycling feedback
        * Contract completion--design continuity and termination

3.   Have each individual provide specific examples regarding each of the six phases. How was contact made? Was a formal contract developed? What specific examples can they provide regarding problem analysis, goal setting, and taking action? How was the contract completed? Have each professional identify tips for success regarding each phase.

4.   Compare and contrast the responses received from each interviewee and hypothesize as to why the responses are similar or different (i.e., is it the result of personal style, occupational setting, the specific situation for which the consulting was performed, etc?).

Acting as a Resource Person in Health Education

Competency B
Establish effective consultive relationships with those requesting assistance in solving health-related problems.

Sub-Competency 1
Analyze parameters of effective consultative relationships.

Activity: How Formal Is It?

Student Outcome: The student can distinguish between formal and informal consultative relationships.

Directions:

1.   There are two types of consultative relationships. With formal consulting, the health educator is viewed as the "expert" and is asked to provide technical expertise. In a more informal consultative relationship, the health educator offers ideas, suggests resources, and provides information.

2.   Read the three scenarios listed below. On a separate sheet of paper, indicate whether a formal or informal consultative relationship is described. Justify your choice.

   a. As a health educator in a high school, you are asked to meet with a committee of teachers and parents who are concerned with the growing gang activity near the school.

              Formal or Informal?   Why?

   b. As a public health educator, you have been hired by the city officials to analyze data collected in a large-scale needs assessment.

              Formal or Informal?   Why?

   c. As a high school teacher, your principal asks you to develop and implement a peer mediation program in the school.

              Formal or Informal?   Why?

3.   Now select any one of the five health education settings (community, medical, post-secondary, school, worksite). Discuss a situation in which a formal consultative relationship may be established. Then describe an informal consultative relationship situation.

Acting as a Resource Person in Health Education

Competency B
Establish effective consultive relationships with those requesting assistance in solving health-related problems.

Sub-Competency 2
Describe special skills and abilities needed by health educators for consultation activities.

Activity: Comparing Perceived And Actual Consultative Skills And Abilities

Student Outcome: After interviewing prospective and professional health educators via electronic mail, the student can describe perceived and actual skills and abilities needed by health educators for performing consultative work.

Directions:

1.   Develop a brief, one paragraph advertisement requesting responses by students in health education to the question, "What special skills and abilities are needed by health educators for consultative activities?" Next ask, "Can you recommend one consultant to interview and supply that person's name and e-mail address?" Include your name, university affiliation, e-mail address, and a request for responses by a given date.

2.   Post the ad on the Student HEDIR. (See "Getting Started" for instructions on subscribing to the Student HEDIR.)

3.   Compile the responses you receive and write a summary of the perceived skills and abilities needed for consultative work as mentioned by the students.

4.   Arrange an e-mail interview with a health education professional who performs consultative work (if possible, use the consultants referred from the Student HEDIR interviews). Ask the same question, "What special skills and abilities are needed by health educators for consultative activities?" If no names and e-mail addresses come from the Student HEDIR interviews, check with faculty in your health education department for the names of consultants and contact them.

5.   Compile the responses from the professional and write a summary of the skills and abilities needed for consultative activities.

6.   Compare the two summaries and identify differences in perceived and actual skills and abilities.

<u>Getting Started</u>

To subscribe to the Student HEDIR, send an e-mail message to Listserv@siu.edu. Skip the subject section, and type Subscribe HEDIRS-L Your Name. After sending it to SIU's listserv, you will receive a memo indicating that you are now subscribed to the listserv. To unsubscribe, send an e-mail to the above address, skip the subject section, and type Unsubscribe HEDIRS-L Your Name. Again, you will receive a memo indicating that you have been unsubscribed.

Acting as a Resource Person in Health Education

Competency B
Establish effective consultive relationships with those requesting assistance in solving health-related problems.

Sub-Competency 2
Describe special skills and abilities needed by health educators for consultation activities.

Activity: Consulting Skills

Student Outcome: The student can explain how health educators are professionally prepared to serve as consultants.

Directions:

1.   Review the responsibilities, competencies, and subcompetencies of Certified Health Education Specialists (CHES) as published by the National Commission for Health Education Credentialing, Inc.

2.   On a separate sheet of paper, identify those skills necessary for serving as a health consultant.

3.   In addition, what experiences prepare health educators to serve as consultants?

Getting Started

For a list of the responsibilities, competencies, and subcompetencies of certified health education specialists, see the Appendix. For your own copy, write to:

National Commission for Health Education Credentialing, Inc.
944 Marcon Blvd., Suite 310
Allentown, PA 18103
(601) 264-8200
(800) 813-0727 (fax)
cogs101w@wonder.em.cdc.gov (e-mail)

Acting as a Resource Person in Health Education

Competency B
Establish effective consultive relationships with those requesting assistance in solving health-related problems.

Sub-Competency 3
Formulate a plan for providing consultation to other health professionals.

Activity: Asking The Right Questions

Student Outcome: The student can list appropriate questions to be asked when engaging in consultative activities.

Directions:

1. Consider the following scenario:

    The Itasca County Hospital Board of Directors wants to form partnerships with the community to expand health education programming and services throughout the county. You have been hired as a consultant to guide them in assessing needs, planning, implementing, evaluating, and coordinating programs.

2. Using six of the seven areas of responsibility for a health educator as a guide, develop a list of questions a consultant would want to have answered in order to meet Itasca County Hospital's goal of expanding community health education programming and services.

3. Add your questions to the list on the following pages.

Notes

ASKING THE RIGHT QUESTIONS

Needs Assessment

1. What specific problems is the community experiencing?

2. What kinds of programs/services are needed?

3.

4.

5.

Program Planning

1. How have previous programs and services worked?

2. Who are the key community decision-makers and gatekeepers to involve in the planning process?

3.

4.

5.

Program Implementation

1. Is the hospital the most appropriate agency to respond to community needs?

2. What assistance can be identified to help implement programs? (e.g., funding, personnel, resources)

3.

4.

5.

ASKING THE RIGHT QUESTIONS - CON'T.

Program Evaluation

1. What types of evaluation should be used to assess achievement of program goals and objectives?

2. What types of data should be collected to assess program effectiveness?

3.

4.

5.

Coordinating

1. What agencies/organizations in the county have similar missions and goals?

2. How can the agencies/organizations best collaborate?

3.

4.

5.

Communicating

1. Is a computerized health information retrieval system available?

2. What are the most effective and efficient means of communicating with county residents? (e.g., word of mouth, newspaper, radio, TV)

3.

4.

5.

Acting as a Resource Person in Health Education

Competency B
Establish effective consultive relationships with those requesting assistance in solving health-related problems.

Sub-Competency 3
Formulate a plan for providing consultation to other health professionals.

Activity: Defining The Consultant's Role

Student Outcome: The student can explain ways of developing satisfying consultative relationships.

Directions:

1.   Imagine that you have been contacted by a local public health department to act as a consultant on a violence prevention grant.

2.   To date, you have received only a phone message inquiring about your interest and availability to serve as a consultant.

3.   In groups of two or three, develop a list of questions you want to ask about your role as a consultant on the grant. For example:

   a. What is the time frame for the grant?
   b. Is this a paid or unpaid position?

4.   List at least five more questions that will help you define your role as a consultant and help you make a decision.

5.   If time allows, different groups can share their questions to look for similarities and differences.

Acting as a Resource Person in Health Education

Competency B
Establish effective consultive relationships with those requesting assistance in solving health-related problems.

Sub-Competency 4
Explain the process of marketing health education consultative services.

Activity: Interview With A Health Education Consultant

Student Outcome: After interviewing at least one health education consultant, the student can explain how a health education consultant might market his/her services.

Directions:

1.   Contact at least one health education consultant and request an interview about the marketing process for consultative services.

2.   From the interview, determine where, when, and how that person publicizes his/her services.

3.   Based upon the results of the interview, write a summary of the marketing process for consultative services.

Getting Started

Use any of the following means by which to locate the names, addresses, phone numbers, or e-mail addresses of health education consultants:

1.   Health Education Student Directory (listserv): Advertise for the name and e-mail address of a health education consultant. To subscribe to the Student HEDIR, send an e-mail message to listserv@SIU.edu. Skip the subject section, and type "Subscribe HEDIRS-L Your Name." After you send it to SIUs listserv, you will receive a memo indicating that you are now subscribed.
2.   Program from a state and/or national conference: Health education consultants often are identified in the listing of conference participants.
3.   Check with faculty in your department who do consulting work; they may be able to help you or refer you to others.

Acting as a Resource Person in Health Education

Competency B
Establish effective consultive relationships with those requesting assistance in solving health-related problems.

Sub-Competency 4
Explain the process of marketing health education consultative services.

Activity: "Marketing Yourself"

Student Outcome: The student can assess his/her potential as a future consultant by identifying current health education skills.

Directions:

1.   If you have a current resume, you may use it for this assignment. If not, this assignment will assist you in developing a resume for future use.

2.   On the worksheet that follows, there are four categories of experiences that have helped you build health education skills.

3.   Under each category, identify the experiences you have had to date. Under each experience, identify one, two, or more skills that you have acquired as a result. Try to use action verbs to better describe your skills. For example:

   Certifications
   HIV/AIDS Instructor, American Red Cross   1994 to Present
         * Present HIV information in culturally sensitive manner
         * Facilitate controversial questions and issues
         * Maintain resource file with latest medical advances

4.   You may wish to consult the listing of health education skills outlined in the Appendix.

Notes

MARKETING YOURSELF

Relevant Work Experience

    Job Title   Dates of Employment

Volunteer Experiences

    Agency/Organization   Date(s)

Certifications/Special Trainings

    Type of Training   Date Received

Computer Skills

    Type of Skill

Notes

Acting as a Resource Person in Health Education

Competency C
Interpret and respond to requests for health information.

Sub-Competency 1
Analyze general processes for identifying the information needed to satisfy a request.

Activity: Interpreting Results

Student Outcome: The student can identify the components of a complete and clear request for health information.

Directions:

1.   As a health educator, you often will be asked to locate health information upon request. For this activity, imagine that you are completing an internship at the American Cancer Society.

2.   The attached letter is received in the mail and your supervisor asks you to complete the request.

3.   Identify the problems with this letter. Circle the sections in which more information is needed.

4.   Rewrite the letter, adding to and clarifying the request based upon your analysis. Submit your work to the instructor.

Getting Started

Brock, S. L. (1988). Better business writing (rev. ed.). Los Altos, CA: Crisp.

American Cancer Society
1234 Normal Lane
Springfield, IL

To Whom It May Concern:

I need your help in getting information for a class that I am taking. Please send all your information on cancer that is available from your agency. I would appreciate it if you could send it as soon as possible. Please call me if you have questions about my request.
Thank you for your help.

Sincerely,

John Smith
2209 Douglas Hall
Southwestern Illinois University
Belleville, IL

Acting as a Resource Person in Health Education

Competency C
Interpret and respond to requests for health information.

Sub-Competency 1
Analyze general processes for identifying the information needed to satisfy a request.

Activity: Patient Education Referral

Student Outcome: The student can describe factors to consider in interpreting a request for health information.

Directions:

1.   Read the following scenario:

        You are a health education intern working for the hospital's patient education department. In your mailbox one morning you find a request for a list of resources for family members of a patient who has been diagnosed as being in the early stages of Alzheimer's disease. The nurse who made the request on behalf of the family members is off duty.

2.   Make a list of additional information you would like to have before responding to this request.

3.   Assuming that the additional information will not be available before you need to compile a list for the patient, explain the steps you would take to gather appropriate information.

Acting as a Resource Person in Health Education

Competency C
Interpret and respond to requests for health information.

Sub-Competency 2
Employ a wide range of approaches in referring requesters to valid sources
of health information.

Activity: Knowing Your Resources

Student Outcome: The student can identify multiple resources that will assist in referring individuals to appropriate sources for health information.

Directions:

1.   Imagine that you are a health educator employed in a setting in which you receive numerous requests for sources of health information.

2.   Select a topic area in health education. Try to identify a specific topic, such as "acquaintance rape" rather than violence, or "radon" rather than environment.

3.   Assume a community member calls you and asks for referrals to at least four valid sources of information on the specified topic. She is willing to contact the sources, but wants your assistance in identifying valid ones.

4.   On the worksheet that follows, first identify the topic area. Next, identify appropriate information for each of the four health information sources. Include complete information, such as name, address, phone number, fax number, e-mail address, and ordering information.

Getting Started

You may wish to write for a copy of Health Hotlines. Send a letter of request to:

DIRLINE Information
Specialized Information Services
National Library of Medicine
8600 Rockville Pike
Bethesda, MD 20894

KNOWING YOUR RESOURCES

Topic Area: _____

Valid Internet sources (identify name and *uniform remote locator [URL]*):

Toll-free numbers (provide name of agency and phone number):

Voluntary agency or community agency that may have information on topic (provide name, address, and phone number):

Professional journal article or reliable book that provides information on the topic (include complete reference information):

Notes

Acting as a Resource Person in Health Education

Competency C
Interpret and respond to requests for health information.

Sub-Competency 2
Employ a wide range of approaches in referring requesters to valid sources
of health information.

Activity: Chlamydia Is Not A Flower! Referral Approaches

Student Outcome: The student can list several approaches to a request for information about
a specific health concern (chlamydia).

Directions:

1.   Consider the following scenario: A student in your dorm or apartment building knows
        you are a prospective health educator and asks you several questions about chlamydia.
        Because it is apparent that the student knows very little about chlamydia, you make
        several recommendations as to where and how that person might find additional
        accurate information about chlamydia.

2.   Think of as many approaches as possible that you might take in responding to that
        person's request for information. List those approaches on the following worksheet.

3.   After you have identified as many approaches as possible, talk with several health
        education students. Ask them for suggestions of additional approaches. Add useful
        ideas to your list.

Notes

CHLAMYDIA IS NOT A FLOWER! REFERRAL APPROACHES

1.

2.

3.

4.

5.

6.

Notes

Acting as a Resource Person in Health Education

Competency D
Select effective educational resource materials for dissemination.

Sub-Competency 1
Assemble educational material of value to the health of individuals
and community groups.

Activity: Health Education Resource File

Student Outcome: The student can develop a resource file of health education information and resources.

Directions:

1.   Use the following categories to identify potential sources of health information and resources:

* Official agencies (government/tax-supported; e.g., Department of Health and Human Services, Centers for Disease Control and Prevention, National Institutes of Health, state and local health departments)
* Voluntary health organizations (e.g., American Cancer Society, American Red Cross)
* Consumer groups (e.g., Better Business Bureau)
* Professional organizations (e.g., American Medical Association, American School Health Association, American Public Health Association, Society of Public Health Educators)
* Philanthropic groups (e.g., Robert Wood Johnson Foundation, Kellogg Foundation, Kaiser Foundation)
* Civic/service groups (e.g., Shriners Club, Lions Club)
* Religious groups (e.g., specific denominations may offer health-related services and/or counseling)

2.   Sources of information to consider and include when appropriate:

* Listing of 800 numbers related to health
* Local directory of health-related agencies
* Internet
* Yellow pages of the telephone book

3.   Write or visit an agency from one of the categories listed above, and request sample pamphlets or brochures that are offered by the agency.

4.   Review materials and determine to what extent items are culturally sensitive, written in technical or lay terminology, and targeted to a specific age group or target population, such as parents or children.

5.   Organize a resource file box for materials. Use of sections identifying major content areas (such as community health, consumer health, environmental health, family life, mental and emotional health, injury prevention and safety, nutrition, personal health, prevention and control of disease, substance use and abuse) is one means for organizing the material.

Getting Started

Purchase a sturdy file box that is large enough to allow for expansion of your resource file as you collect additional information in the next year or two.

Acting as a Resource Person in Health Education

Competency D
Select effective educational resource materials for dissemination.

Sub-Competency 1
Assemble educational material of value to the health of individuals
and community groups.

Activity: Resource Materials Search

Student Outcome: The student can gather health resource materials and identify their appropriateness for specific individuals and groups.

Directions:

1.   As the Director of Health Education at Lakeview County Health Department, you have been assigned the task of gathering resource materials on the following health topics listed below. These materials will be disseminated to clients at the health department:

        * Cardiovascular disease
        * Immunizations
        * Nutrition
        * Radon
        * Sexually transmitted diseases (STDs)

2.   Gather at least five print resource materials on each topic.

3.   For each resource, identify the specific individuals and groups for which the informational material is most appropriate. Justify your choices by using readability formulas, checking currency of information, and determining cultural sensitivity, etc.

Acting as a Resource Person in Health Education

Competency D
Select effective educational resource materials for dissemination.

Sub-Competency 2
Evaluate the worth and applicability of resource materials for given audiences.

Activity: Audiovisual Aid Assessment Practice

Student Outcome: The student can utilize preview forms to determine the worth of audiovisual aids for a given audience.

Directions:

1.   Choose one of the four assessment forms that follow the "Getting Started" section to use in previewing an audiovisual aid, such as a video, film, or slidetape program.

2.   Use the form to decide whether you would purchase or rent the audiovisual aid for the given audience. Your instructor will provide the audiovisual aid for you to preview, and also identify the intended audience.

3.   After previewing the audiovisual aid, discuss in small groups the following areas. First, share with others your decision to use or not use the audiovisual aid. Second, identify reasons for your decision. Third, discuss the value of the assessment form you selected to use in previewing the audiovisual aid. If additional information should be provided on the assessment form, provide ideas on what it should be.

Getting Started

Note: The instructor should facilitate arrangements for an audiovisual aid which students can preview either in class or at a media center on campus. In addition, the instructor should identify the intended audience before students preview the audiovisual aid.

AUDIOVISUAL AID EVALUATION

1) Title:

2) Year of Publication: **3) Length:**

4) Type of Aid:

5) Organizational Source:

    Address:

    Phone:

    Fax:

    E-Mail:

6) Availability:

    ❑ Free   ❑ Loan   ❑ Rental ($_____)   ❑ Purchase ($_____)

7) Specific Subject Area:

8) Target Audience:

9) Appropriate Language Level For Intended Audience:

    ❑ Yes   ❑ No

10) Culturally Diverse:

    ❑ Yes   ❑ No

(over)

11) Supplemental Materials Provided:

❏ Yes   ❏ No

If yes, what types? (model, outline, discussion guide)

12) Additional Comments:

Person Assessing Audiovisual:

Date Assessed:

AUDIOVISUAL AID EVALUATION FORM

1. Title:

2. Length: *(Include hours and minutes)*

3. Date of Production:

4. Specific Subject Area:

5. Target Audience: *(Of Audiovisual Aid)*

6. Type of Audiovisual Aid: *(e.g. Video, Film, CD-Rom, Slide, etc.)*

   * If Slide, is tape included?_____

7. Information on where to Obtain Audiovisual Aid *(If applicable)*:

   Distributor's:
   Name: _____

   Address: _____

   _____

   _____

   Phone: _____

   Fax: _____

   E-mail: _____

CHECKLIST:

Check the corresponding box that applies, and then answer each question that follows.

Yes   No

☐   ☐ Appropriate Language Level

        Why or Why not?_____

Yes   No

☐   ☐ Cultural Diversity Fits Needs

        Why or Why not?_____

Yes   No

☐   ☐ Supplemental Material Included *(e.g. Discussion Guide)*

        If so, what is it?_____

        Usefulness?_____

Availability of Audiovisual Aid: *(more than one may apply)*

    ☐ Free

    ☐ Rental: $_____

    ☐ Purchase: $_____

    ☐ Preview

    ☐ Other: _____

Additional Comments/Information:

_____

_____

_____

_____

Reviewed By:_____ Date:_____

AUDIOVISUAL AID EVALUATION FORM

Descriptive Information
Title of Audiovisual Aid:
Type of Audiovisual Aid (i.e., videotape, CD-ROM, film, slides):
Specific Subject Area:
Date Produced:
Running Time/Length:
Distributing Source:
Distributing Source Address, Phone Number, E-Mail, Fax Number:
Availability & Cost (i.e., free, rent, purchase, preview)

Content Information
Target Audience:
Language & Focus Age-Appropriate for Target Audience:
Cultural Sensitivity & Diversity:
Available Supplemental Materials (i.e., discussion guide, review sheets):

(over)

Production Quality & Usefulness
Message Clear & Meaningful? (briefly explain)
Present-Day Relevance? (briefly explain)
Available in Languages Other than English? (if so, please specify)
PotentiallyValuable Educational Resource for Your Agency? (briefly explain)

Personal Comments of Reviewer

Date of Assessment:	**Reviewed By:**

AUDIOVISUAL EVALUATION FORM

PRODUCT DESCRIPTION

Title of Product: _____

Format: _____

Length: _____

Source Name: _____

Address: _____

City: _____ **State:** _____ **Phone:** _____

Fax Number: _____ **E-Mail:** _____

Producer: _____ **Publication:** _____

Availability:

_____Unknown

_____Available Free

_____Payment Required

_____Price $ _____

_____Free A-V Loan Program

_____Source (if different from above)

List Supplemental Materials: (i.e. study guide) _____

_____

_____

CONTENT DESCRIPTION

Special Subject Area: _____

Description: (In two or three sentences) _____

_____

_____

Target Audience: (Range of appropriate age groups) _____

_____

Cultural Diversity: _____

Language Level: (Is it appropriate for the target audience?)

                    Yes _____   No _____

Briefly explain your response: _____

_____

Length Appropriate:

                    Yes _____   No _____

Briefly explain your response: _____

_____

Additional Comments: _____

_____

Reviewed by: _____

Acting as a Resource Person in Health Education

Competency D
Select effective educational resource materials for dissemination.

Sub-Competency 2
Evaluate the worth and applicability of resource materials for given audiences.

Activity: Resource Evaluation Forms

Student Outcome: The student can identify and locate sample instruments for the purpose of evaluating health education resources.

Directions:

1.   Locate a sample evaluation form, checklist, or assessment criteria for any type of print health education material or resources (pamphlets, brochures, fact sheets or textbooks, packaged curricula, etc.). There are many examples that can be found in the literature.

2.   Use the sample form to evaluate three different resources on the same topic targeted to a specific population. Be sure to select resources that the form is designed to evaluate.

3.   Write a one paragraph summary which describes the resource you think is best and why. Also, include the three completed evaluation forms.

4.   Be sure to properly reference your sample evaluation form.

Getting Started

Most school or community health methods books will have suggestions for evaluating resources, or refer specifically to the following reference:

   Ames, E., Trucano, L., Wan, J., & Harris, M. (1992). Designing health education curricula: Planning for good health. Dubuque, IA: William C. Brown.

Acting as a Resource Person in Health Education

Competency D
Select effective educational resource materials for dissemination.

Sub-Competency 3
Apply various processes in the acquisition of resource materials.

Activity: Costs Of Selected Instructional Materials

Student Outcome: The student can identify various costs associated with a variety of health education resources.

Directions:

1.   Complete the charts on the following page with information about health education resources and their costs.

2.   Contact local voluntary health organizations or find catalogs that sell health education materials.

Getting Started

Ask your instructor, or a community or school health educator to provide names and addresses of companies providing such catalogs.

COSTS OF SELECTED INSTRUCTIONAL MATERIALS

Topic: Nutrition			
Printed Resource			
Title	**Description**	**Cost**	**Contact/Source**
Nutrition for Athletes	Fact Sheets	$10.00/100	National Dairy Council
A-V Resource			
Title	**Description**	**Cost**	**Contact/Source**
Curriculum			
Title	**Description**	**Cost**	**Contact/Source**

Topic: Consumer Health			
Printed Resource			
Title	**Description**	**Cost**	**Contact/Source**
A-V Resource			
Title	**Description**	**Cost**	**Contact/Source**
Curriculum			
Title	**Description**	**Cost**	**Contact/Source**

Topic: Growth and Development			
Printed Resource			
Title	**Description**	**Cost**	**Contact/Source**
A-V Resource			
Title	**Description**	**Cost**	**Contact/Source**
Curriculum			
Title	**Description**	**Cost**	**Contact/Source**

Notes

Acting as a Resource Person in Health Education

Competency D
Select effective educational resource materials for dissemination.

Sub-Competency 3
Apply various processes in the acquisition of resource materials.

<u>Activity: Resources, Where Are They?</u>

Student Outcome: The student can locate potential health resources within a local community.

Directions:

1.   From the following list, choose at least four of the following activities to complete in locating health resources.

   a. Call a local hospital to determine if a health educator or educational specialist is employed. If so, contact that person to discuss availability of resources that are free or on loan to other community health educators.

   b. Talk with a local librarian to identify recent acquisitions in the field of health (i.e., new journal or magazine subscription, new books, videos, or audiotapes).

   c. Visit a retail store which sells computer software to survey the types and costs of health-related software.

   d. Visit or call the local county health department to determine availability of free health materials, such as pamphlets and/or fact sheets.

   e. Write a letter to a voluntary health agency requesting a publications list and order form.

   f. Send for the <u>Health Hotlines</u> publication from the National Institutes of Health to be aware of organizations with toll-free telephone numbers.

   g. Visit a local video rental store to determine availability of free health-related videos.

   h. Check the local public library or post office for a copy of the current <u>Consumer Information Catalog</u> (a catalog of free and low-cost federal publications of consumer interest). If unavailable at these locations, send for one at the following address, or check out the Web site: www.pueblo.gsa.gov

      S. James, Consumer Information Center - 6A, PO Box 100,
      Pueblo, CO 81002

i. Check local library for the following books published by Educators Progress Service, Inc. Each book identifies free materials and the criteria for receiving them.

Educators Guide to Free Films, Filmstrips, and Slides
Educators Guide to Free Teaching Aids
Educators Guide to Free Videotapes
Educators Index of Free Material
Guide to Free Computer Materials

2. Share with classmates your success in finding resources for health education through the selected processes.

Acting as a Resource Person in Health Education

Competency D
Select effective educational resource materials for dissemination.

Sub-Competency 4
Compare different methods for distributing educational materials.

Activity: Different Distribution Channels

Student Outcome: The student can compare different methods for distributing educational materials in terms of context for use, cost effectiveness, and potential problems/concerns.

Directions:

1.   Review the charts that follow which identify various channels that educational materials can be distributed to the general public or to a segment of the general population.

2.   For each chart, generate ideas about each distribution channel in these areas: context for best use of the channel, cost effectiveness of channel, and potential problems/concerns with the channel.

3.   Contact a community health educator to determine channels used most often by the agency for the distribution of materials to the general population or a segment of it. Compare interviewee's reasons given for selected channels to your ideas on the charts.

4.   Summarize findings in writing.

Notes

DIFFERENT DISTRIBUTION CHANNELS

General Population

Channel	Health Fair	Direct Mail	Local Newspaper Insert	Direct Request After Public Service Announcement	Local Public Places	Combined with Fundraising
Context for Best Use						
Cost Effectiveness						
Problems/Concerns						

Segment of Population

Channel	Worksite Payroll Stuffer	Specific Groups (organizations, support groups, etc.)	Health Site (physician's office health program)	Educational Site (schools, health promotion programs)
Context for Best Use				
Cost Effectiveness				
Problems/Concerns				

Notes

Acting as a Resource Person in Health Education

Competency D
Select effective educational resource materials for dissemination.

Sub-Competency 4
Compare different methods for distributing educational materials.

<u>Activity:</u> <u>Gaining Early Support Before Distribution Of Materials</u>

Student Outcome: The student can use written communication to solicit support for a controversial health education program.

Directions:

1.   Health education often involves controversial topics and issues. Before resources and materials can be effectively used, they must be accepted and supported by the consumer and those influencing the consumers (i.e., parents, company officials, community members, school board members, etc.).

2.   Consider the following scenario:

   A task force is attempting to get a family planning clinic established within the community.

   a. List below some of the groups or individuals who may present obstacles to the idea:

   b. List below some of the reasons you think these individuals or groups might provide as a basis for their opposition:

3.   Write a letter to the editor of the local newspaper that would support the establishment of the clinic. Be careful to avoid offending the opposition. You want to gain their respect and confidence in order to gain their support.

Notes

Glossary of Terms

Agricola: database from the National Agricultural Library focusing on agricultural and nutritional information from journals, government documents, and pamphlets

Center for Health Promotion and Education: clearinghouse sponsored by the Centers for Disease Control and Prevention providing information, resources, and program direction for disease prevention, risk reduction, and health promotion

Clearinghouse on Health Indexes: sponsored by the National Center for Health Statistics, this clearinghouse focuses on information for health researchers, program planners, and the administrative aspect of health

Combined Health Information Database (CHID): health education and health promotion resources (organizations, publications, and programs) available through the Center for Health Promotion and Education of the Centers for Disease Control and Prevention

consultation: a process involving an expert sharing recommendations or services to an interested party

Druginfo: University of Minnesota's Drug Information Services database providing references to drug and alcohol use, as well as abuse and treatment

Educational Resources Information Center (ERIC): database providing journals, articles, unpublished manuscripts, reports, and books focusing on all aspects of education

home page: the first page displayed when a web site is accessed; it typically provides an introduction to the site and provides links to various documents stored at the site

link: a connection to another part of the document that elaborates on the word or phrase that constituted the link

MEDLINE: database from the National Library of Medicine that references journals in biomedicine, science, and allied health fields

Medical and Psychological Previews: weekly updates of citations from articles, editorials, and letters found in medical and psychological journals

National Health Information Center: formerly the National Health Information Clearinghouse, this Office of Disease Prevention and Health Promotion Clearinghouse refers the inquirer to appropriate health information resources

PsycINFO: formerly Psychological Abstracts, the American Psychological Association's references to articles, monographs, dissertations, and reports from the psychological and behavioral sciences

search engine: a program available on the Internet which locates sources by subject; examples include Webcrawler and Yahoo

Sports Database: Canadian database produced by the Sport Information Resource Centre of Ontario providing citations to sources covering sports medicine, athletics, and recreation

Student HEDIR: Health Education Directory listserv available for students

uniform remote locator (URL): the address of each resource (file) on the Internet; it consists of the name of the computer system where the resource is stored, the directory path to the specific resource, and the file name

References

Deeds, S. G., Cleary, M. J., & Neiger, B. L. (Eds.). (1996). <u>The certified health education specialist: A self-study guide for professional competency.</u> Allentown, PA: National Commission for Health Education Credentialing.

National Commission for Health Education Credentialing, Inc. (1996). <u>A competency-based framework for professional development of certified health education specialists.</u> Allentown, PA: Author.

Simons-Morton, B., Greene, W., & Gottlieb, N. (1995). <u>Introduction to health education and health promotion.</u> Prospect Heights, IL: Waveland.

U.S. Department of Health and Human Services. (1991). <u>Healthy people 2000: National health promotion and disease prevention objectives.</u> Washington, DC: Government Printing Office.

Notes

7 *Communicating Health and Health Education Needs, Concerns, and Resources*

Downie, Fyfe, and Tannahill (1990) define health education as "communication activity aimed at enhancing positive health and preventing or diminishing ill health in individuals and groups, through influencing the beliefs, attitudes, and behavior of those with power and of the community at large" (p. 28). Therefore, communication is a vital component in the prevention of disease and promotion of health through behavior change. "Health messages about health risks and benefits, based firmly in science and presented with sensitivity to the consumer, are crucial to motivate such change" (Roper, 1993, p. 179). If successfully delivered, communication can (National Cancer Institute, 1992):

* increase awareness of a health issue, problem, or solution
* affect attitudes to create support for individual or collective action
* demonstrate or illustrate skills
* increase demand for health services
* remind about or reinforce knowledge, attitudes, or behavior (p. 1)

A discipline exists which focuses solely on health communication. The health communication discipline is multidisciplinary by design, including principles based in communication, *social marketing*, *behavioral psychology*, medicine, management, government, education, and public health, among others (Ratzan, 1994). Health communication is defined as "the crafting and delivery of messages and strategies, based on consumer research, to promote the health of individuals and communities" (Roper, 1993, p. 181). Therefore, "health communication programs can be designed to inform, influence, and motivate institutional or public audiences" (National Cancer Institute, 1992, p. 1).

Health communication programs must be based on an understanding of the needs and perceptions of their target audiences. Therefore, the health educator must have an understanding of needs assessment, as well as program planning, implementation, and evaluation to ensure the success of a health communication program.

The health educator also needs to understand the various *models* related to the design and development of health communication programs. A seven-step model, suggested by McGuire (1984) focuses on the design of public health communication campaigns. The Health Communication Wheel, a ten-step model developed by the Centers for Disease Control, focuses on the need to incorporate health communication into prevention strategies (Roper, 1993). The National Cancer Institute's (1992) six-step model is most useful for developing communication activities through both *mass media* and printed materials (other than newspapers).

Also, the health educator must be capable of selecting various communication methods and techniques in providing health information to diverse populations. This may include the delivery of health messages through verbal, written, and *graphic* means. This involves competence in working with the media, computers, and networking with others within and outside the field of health education.

Fostering communication between health care providers and consumers is vital. Comprehending health care providers' messages and being able to relay them to consumers is an essential part of ensuring that the population has a broad base of knowledge.

Not only must the health educator be capable of communicating information about health to diverse populations, but must also be capable of explaining the foundations of the health education discipline and the major responsibilities of health educators to others outside the field of health education (National Commission for Health Education Credentialing

[NCHEC], 1996). This is imperative to the existence and advancement of the health education profession.

Health communication is an essential component in disease prevention and health promotion strategies. In the next few paragraphs, specific examples of the communication process occurring in a variety of health education settings is provided.

Community Health Setting

A consumer health presentation will be delivered to a community service organization. The health educator identifies communication techniques appropriate for providing information to the group. Specific considerations for presenting information in verbal, written, and graphic formats is reviewed. The health educator chooses to use written handouts, slides of charts and graphs, and group discussion in presenting the informational material.

Medical Setting

The health educator at a local health maintenance organization (HMO) is planning a communication campaign regarding health nutritional practices for the HMO clients. Factors are examined to determine how the information will best be assimilated. The health educator chooses a panel and discussion approach for an evening program on nutritional disorders. The panel includes a well-respected physician, diabetes educator, and registered dietitian. As part of the campaign strategies, the health educator identifies posters, table tents, and a newsletter with humorous, helpful hints for incorporating good nutritional practices into one's busy life. Finally, brochures are selected on decreasing fat, sodium, and sugar intake, and increasing fiber intake which will be available throughout the HMO facility.

Post-Secondary Setting

Peer health educators working with the university staff health educators are developing a communication campaign to be held during Alcohol Awareness Week. It is decided that the messages must be factual, attention-getting, and brief. *Public service announcements* on local radio and television, editorials in the school and city newspapers, table tents in local taverns, a victim impact panel presentation, and a mock DUI are chosen as methods to convey the awareness messages.

School Setting

The health education curriculum at a local junior high is in danger of being eliminated. The principal asks the health educator to defend the need for health education to the school board. In developing the presentation, the health educator includes an explanation of the field of health education, its goals, and common methodologies. To enhance the presentation, the health educator includes transparencies indicating the health status of the students, a videotape of a class role-playing activity, and handouts indicating the scope and sequence of the health education curriculum.

Worksite Setting

A factory has encountered a significant increase in work-related accidents during the third shift of operation. Management encourages and supports the development of a safety program to reduce the number of accidents and days of work lost due to accidents. Management personnel asks the health educator to explain management's concern for the employees' health and well-being to the shift supervisors and its correlation to cost-effectiveness. Acting as a *liaison*, the health educator will relay concerns and questions from the shift supervisors to the management level regarding the safety program.

Communicating Health and Health Education Needs, Concerns, and Resources

Competency A
Interpret concepts, purposes, and theories of health education.

Sub-Competency 1
Evaluate the state-of-the-art of health education.

Activity: Health Education: A Plethora Of Definitions

Student Outcome: The student can compare a variety of traditional definitions of health education and develop a "personal" definition of health education.

Directions:

1.   Review the literature on health education and find at least five different definitions for the term "health education." Use some of the works listed in "Getting Started."

2.   Identify key words or phrases in each definition that you think are the best descriptors of health education.

3.   Use the chart on the next page to organize your findings.

4.   Finally, using the key words and phrases you identified in step two, construct your own definition of health education using the space provided on the next page.

Getting Started

Anspaugh, D. J., & Ezell, G. (1995). Teaching today's health (4th ed.). Boston: Allyn and Bacon.

Bedworth, D. A., & Bedworth, A. E. (1992). The profession and practice of health education. Dubuque, IA: Wm. C. Brown.

Green, L. W., Krueter, M. W., Deeds, S. G., & Partridge, K. B. (1980). Health education planning: A diagnostic approach. Palo Alto, CA: Mayfield.

Joint Commission on Health Education Terminology. (1973). Health Education Monographs, 33, 63-70.

Notes

HEALTH EDUCATION: A PLETHORA OF DEFINITIONS

Source	Definition	Key Words/Phrases

PERSONAL DEFINITION OF HEALTH EDUCATION

Your Name _____

My definition of health education is

Notes

Communicating Health and Health Education Needs, Concerns, and Resources

Competency A
Interpret concepts, purposes, and theories of health education.

Sub-Competency 1
Evaluate the state-of-the-art of health education.

Activity: "State-Of-The-Art" Article

Student Outcome: The student can articulate, in the form of a written article, the current state-of-the-art of health education in the United States.

Directions:

1.   As a member of the state health education association, you are asked to write a feature article for the student issue of the association newsletter. You have been asked to describe the state-of-the-art of health education in the U.S. in 600 words or less.

2.   Indicate how you would go about preparing for the article's content, such as where you would locate reference and resource information to use in the article.

3.   Type out a draft of the article with all key points included.

4.   Give your draft to a faculty member, or send a copy to the editor of the state health education association for feedback. After revising, you may wish to submit the written product to the state health association newsletter.

Getting Started

As a stylistic and content reference, consult the following:

Seffrin, J. R. (1990). The comprehensive school health curriculum: Closing the gap between state-of-the-art and state-of-the-practice. Journal of School Health, 60 (4), 151-156.

Communicating Health and Health Education Needs, Concerns, and Resources

Competency A
Interpret concepts, purposes, and theories of health education.

Sub-Competency 2
Analyze the foundations of the discipline of health education.

<u>Activity: The Credentialing Journey</u>

Student Outcome: The student can provide a historical overview of the events and people involved in the credentialing process.

Directions:

1.   Research the credentialing process in health education.

2.   Using the chart on the following page, identify the key events, individual leaders, and supportive organizations instrumental to the evolution of the current credentialing process of Certified Health Education Specialists.

3.   In addition, in the space provided, briefly indicate why you think health education specialists should or should not be certified.

THE CREDENTIALING JOURNEY

Date	Event	Key People	Organization

CERTIFICATION OF HEALTH EDUCATION SPECIALISTS

Briefly explain why you think health education specialists should or should not be certified?

Notes

Communicating Health and Health Education Needs, Concerns, and Resources

Competency A
Interpret concepts, purposes, and theories of health education.

Sub-Competency 2
Analyze the foundations of the discipline of health education.

Activity: Using Health Education Foundations In A Job Interview

Student Outcome: The student can analyze the foundations of health education.

Directions:

1.   Consider the following scenario:

   You have been notified that you are one of three candidates for an entry level position as a drug and alcohol prevention specialist with the Department of Mental Health. You are aware that the educational training backgrounds of the other two candidates are social work and psychology. (If this scenario would never apply to you, then respond to it as if you have a friend who is applying and you are giving your friend advice.)

2.   Given the above information, prepare a concise analysis of the foundations of health education to demonstrate you are the most qualified for the position.

3.   On a separate sheet of paper, prepare an outline of what you want to include in your interview discussion about the foundations of health education.

4.   If possible, share your outline with the internship supervisor in your department. Ask for suggestions on how to strengthen your presentation about the foundations of health education to prospective employers in practical and meaningful terminology.

Getting Started

For helpful information on foundations of health education, consult the following:

Bedworth, A. E., & Bedworth, D. A. (1992). The profession and practice of health education. Dubuque, IA: William C. Brown.

Butler, J. T. (1997). Principles of health education and health promotion (2nd ed.). Englewood, CO: Morton.

Simons-Morton, B. G., Greene, W. H., & Gottlieb, N. H. (1995). Introduction to health education and health promotion (2nd ed.). Prospect Heights, IL: Waveland.

Communicating Health and Health Education Needs, Concerns, and Resources

Competency A
Interpret concepts, purposes, and theories of health education.

Sub-Competency 3
Describe major responsibilities of the health educator in the practice of health education.

Activity: Marketing What We Do

Student Outcome: The student can describe the various responsibility areas of a health educator.

Directions:

1.   Consider the following scenario: The local board of health lacks understanding of the profession of health education which prevents them from acknowledging health educators as qualified candidates for health education positions. They consistently choose to hire candidates with nursing or dietetics degrees. You have been asked by the health department administrator to prepare a letter to the board members explaining the responsibilities of practicing health educators.

2.   Write a two page letter encouraging the board to consider health educators as viable candidates for positions at the health department.

3.   In the letter explain the responsibilities of health educators and indicate the range of skills and roles of a practicing health educator.

4.   Keep the letter to two pages to maintain readers' interest.

Getting Started

The National Commission for Health Education Credentialing, Inc. (1996). A competency-based framework for professional development of certified health education specialists. Allentown, PA: Author.

Communicating Health and Health Education Needs, Concerns, and Resources

Competency A
Interpret concepts, purposes, and theories of health education.

Sub-Competency 3
Describe major responsibilities of the health educator in the practice of health education.

Activity: Exploring Objectives By Category

Student Outcome: The student can distinguish among health promotion, disease prevention, and disease control.

Directions:

1.   Obtain a copy or summary of Healthy People 2000: National Health Promotion and Disease Prevention Objectives from your instructor or library.

2.   Review the objectives from a topic area (e.g., sexually transmitted diseases, oral health) or population of your choice (e.g., adolescents, older adults).

3.   Use the chart on the following page to organize the objectives into the categories of health promotion, disease prevention, and disease control. Copy at least one objective for your selected topic or population in the space provided that you believe best represents the area of promotion, prevention, or control.

4.   Below the chart, explain in your own words the differences among health promotion, disease prevention, and disease control.

Notes

EXPLORING OBJECTIVES BY CATEGORY

Topic/Population:

Category	Objective
Health Promotion	
Disease Prevention	
Disease Control	

Health Promotion:

Disease Prevention:

Disease Control:

Notes

Communicating Health and Health Education Needs, Concerns, and Resources

Competency B
Predict the impact of societal value systems on health education programs.

Sub-Competency 1
Investigate social forces causing opposing viewpoints regarding health education needs and concerns.

Activity: <u>Handling Controversial Issues</u>

Student Outcome: The student can state policies and procedures for dealing with controversial issues or guest speakers in schools.

Directions:

1.   Contact the administrative office of a local school or talk to a teacher with whom you are familiar and ask for a copy of the policy and procedures which address controversial issues or guest speakers.

2.   In writing, respond to the following questions:

   a. What constitutes a "controversial issue?"

   b. What restrictions are placed on classroom teachers in discussing the issue?

   c. Who has final approval for allowing a controversial issue to be addressed or a controversial guest speaker to address students?

   d. What, if any, procedures are in place that allow or permit students the option of not being present for the issue or speaker?

   e. In what ways, if any, are parents notified of controversial issues or speakers?

3.   Suggest at least five health issues that probably fall in the "controversial issues" category for schools.

Communicating Health and Health Education Needs, Concerns, and Resources

Competency B
Predict the impact of societal value systems on health education programs.

Sub-Competency 1
Investigate social forces causing opposing viewpoints regarding health education needs and concerns.

Activity: Resolving Opposing Points Of View

Student Outcome: The student can express and support personal views on a controversial issue while acknowledging opposing viewpoints held by others.

Directions:

1.   Select one of the two scenarios described below depending on your interests.

   a. You are a school health educator in a high school that is in the process of reviewing human sexuality curricula for adoption. There is a concern raised by many parents as to whether the curriculum will be strictly abstinence-based or whether other alternatives will be part of the curriculum.

   b. As a health educator at a university health service, you receive grant money to develop an educational program designed to reduce drinking and driving among college students. The grant requires an Advisory Group which consists of students, faculty, and support staff. The Advisory Group members are divided on whether the program should address "designated drivers and responsible drinking" or a program that has a "no drinking" message, since many college students are not of legal age.

2.   Develop either a letter that will be mailed to the parents of the high schoolers or a memorandum to members of the Advisory Group. Within this communication, address the following points:

   a. Describe the variety of viewpoints on this issue and express that all points of view are valued and will be considered.
   b. Address the issue of competing and conflicting personal values which may be the reason for many different viewpoints.
   c. Conclude the memo by asking for ways that others can share their views (perhaps an open meeting of all concerned, e-mail, etc.).

Getting Started

Most word processing software programs provide templates for memorandums or business letters. You may want to utilize these templates for this assignment to develop proficiency in producing a business communication.

Communicating Health and Health Education Needs, Concerns, and Resources

Competency B
Predict the impact of societal value systems on health education programs.

Sub-Competency 2
Employ a wide range of strategies for dealing with controversial health issues.

Activity: Setting Ground Rules

Student Outcome: The student can develop and explain to a group of high school age participants a set of *ground rules* which supports an environment of respect and minimizes disruptive controversy.

Directions:

1.   As either a school health educator or community health educator, you are going to conduct an hour long educational program on HIV/AIDS to a group of high school students.

2.   You plan to use group discussion and other learning methods in a non-judgmental and culturally sensitive learning environment.

3.   Establish a set of ground rules that will be explained to the group as the program begins. List at least five different rules that you want the group to follow. In addition to identifying each rule, provide a brief explanation of the purpose of the rule. (See "Getting Started" for an example.)

4.   Finally, imagine that one of the group participants violates a ground rule. Describe how you, as the facilitator, will handle the situation.

Getting Started

Ground Rule Number One: All persons have the right to express their opinions.

Explanation: When there is a controversial issue, many people have strong opinions. In our activities today, we will respect each other. Each person will be able to express his/her thoughts and opinions. Secondly, to "cut down" or "bad mouth" a person at any time is not acceptable.

Communicating Health and Health Education Needs, Concerns, and Resources

Competency B
Predict the impact of societal value systems on health education programs.

Sub-Competency 2
Employ a wide range of strategies for dealing with controversial health issues.

<u>Activity: Planning Ahead To Prevent/Deal With Controversy</u>

Student Outcome: The student can offer several examples of how to implement strategies for dealing with controversial issues in health education.

Directions:

1.   Determine the health setting in which you plan to seek employment as your frame of reference.

2.   Using one index card for each strategy, record several examples of how each of the following strategies for "preventing controversy" might be implemented in the setting of your choice.

* assure broad-based planning at the local level
* be positive
* do your homework
* make community aware of the need for health education
* seek support
* select articulate spokespersons
* state goals clearly

3.   Again, using one index card for each of the following strategies, list several examples of how each strategy might be employed in the setting of your choice once controversy has developed.

* be honest
* don't get defensive
* keep supporters involved and informed
* know and be able to communicate program goals positively and effectively
* listen to opposition and find common ground
* remain positive
* respect differences you have with the opposition

Source for strategies:

Jackie G. Sowers. (1990). Sowers Associates, One Park Avenue, Hampton, NH. (Handout.) Used with permission.

Communicating Health and Health Education Needs, Concerns, and Resources

Competency C
Select a variety of communication methods and techniques in providing health information.

Sub-Competency 1
Utilize a wide range of techniques for communicating health and health education information.

Activity: Communication Choices

Student Outcome: The student can utilize a range of communication techniques in a health education setting.

Directions:

1.   For two of the communication techniques listed below, describe possible situations for use during the time period from assessing needs for health education through the evaluation phase.

2.   Discuss advantages and disadvantages in utilizing each communication technique.

3.   Finally, describe what needs to be known before successfully utilizing the technique. For example, when writing a business letter, what are the current acceptable styles, what are the major components of a business letter, and why use written communication instead of personal contact? Or, when writing radio public service announcements, what is the preferred time line to follow in sending a PSA to a local radio station, and to whom is the PSA sent?

Audiovisual Aid	Electronic Mail	*Marquee*	Public Service
Advertisement	Fact Sheet	Memorandum	Announcement (PSA)
Billboard	Fax	Newsletter	(Radio/Television)
Booklet/Brochure	Feature Article	Poster	Radio Interview
Bulletin Board	*Flier*	Presentation	Television Interview
Business Letter	*Flip Chart*	*Press Release*	

Getting Started

Brock, S. L. (1988). Better business writing (rev.ed.). Los Altos, CA: Crisp.

Mandel, S. (1994). Technical presentation skills (rev. ed.). Menlo Park, CA: Crisp.

Raines, C. (1989). Visual aids in business. Los Altos, CA: Crisp.

Wade, J. (1992). Dealing effectively with the media. Los Altos, CA: Crisp.

Communicating Health and Health Education Needs, Concerns, and Resources

Competency C
Select a variety of communication methods and techniques in providing health information.

Sub-Competency 1
Utilize a wide range of techniques for communicating health and health education information.

Activity: Communication Methods Exploration

Student Outcome: The student can explain the appropriateness of various communication methods for diverse populations and topics.

Directions:

1.   The following groups and topics will be used for this activity:

   * Inner city seventh grade students enrolled in a drug resistance program
   * Factory laborers enrolled in a worksite heart health program
   * Participants in a senior citizen center course on injury prevention

2.   Identify which of the following communication methods you would utilize for the groups and topics noted above:

   * Interpersonal communication
        - Face-to-face (e.g., peers, family members, health care professional-to-patient)
        - Group delivery (e.g., worksite or classroom)
   * Mass media (e.g., radio, television, magazines, direct mail, billboards, newspapers)
   * Community (e.g., libraries, employers, schools, malls, health fairs, local government agencies)

3.   Explain in class the reasoning for your choices. Describe the effectiveness of these methods for the groups/topics chosen.

Getting Started

National Cancer Institute. (1992). Making health communication programs work: A planner's guide (NIH Publication No. 92-1493/t068). Bethesda, MD: Author.

Communicating Health and Health Education Needs, Concerns, and Resources

Competency C
Select a variety of communication methods and techniques in providing health information.

Sub-Competency 2
Demonstrate proficiency in communicating health information and health education needs.

Activity: Adjustments And Alterations

Student Outcome: The student can describe the use of verbal, written, and graphic health-related information for various population groups.

Directions:

1.   You have been asked to provide presentations to the following population groups:

        * suburban, elementary school students
        * participants in a fitness program for women over 40 years of age
        * unemployed factory workers
        * HMO health care providers

2.   You must incorporate verbal, written, and graphic presentation of information.

3.   Describe the special considerations involved in effectively presenting in each of the three formats. Examples include: certain populations may need large print handouts or brochures due to decreased visual acuity; technical language needs to be evaluated for use with specific groups; attention spans of some groups may be shorter than for others.

Getting Started

Gilbert, G. G., & Sawyer, R. G. (1995). Health education: Creating strategies for school and community health. Boston: Jones and Bartlett.

Communicating Health and Health Education Needs, Concerns, and Resources

Competency C
Select a variety of communication methods and techniques in
providing health information.

Sub-Competency 2
Demonstrate proficiency in communicating health information and health education needs.

Activity: Practice For Communication Proficiency

Student Outcome: The student can communicate the same information to a variety of
individuals, including those being served and those providing services.

Directions:

1.   Working as a health educator in the local health department, you have need to
       communicate with those in your community about a new program, "Women and Heart
       Disease," that will be implemented eight weeks from today. A decision has
       been made by an advisory group working with you to contact both health care
       professionals and women residing in your town. Letters to local physicians and
       hospital administrators plus a press release, radio (15 second and 20 second) public
       service announcements, and fliers are the chosen communication methods.

2.   Write a business letter appropriate for medical personnel and community health
       educators which announces and describes the upcoming program. Ask a peer to
       critique your letter; revise it if necessary.

3.   Select one of the three communication methods mentioned in step one to inform the
       target audience of the new program. Develop the selected technique and, again, ask a
       peer to review and critique your work. Make improvements to your work if needed.

4.   Submit both items to your instructor.

Communicating Health and Health Education Needs, Concerns, and Resources

Competency D
Foster communication between health care providers and consumers.

Sub-Competency 1
Identify the significance and implications of health care providers' messages to consumers.

<u>Activity:</u> <u>Health Updates And Breakthroughs</u>

Student Outcome: The student can compare the media's message with the health care provider's message to the consumer.

Directions:

1.   Often, a major breakthrough in a health-related area is covered in the national and local news. Because of time constraints and editing styles of media personnel, the public may receive partial information. In some cases, the media message may be over-emphasized, give false hope, or even misinform the listeners by omitting pertinent information. Find a recent example of a health update or breakthrough, such as tests for early diagnosis of Alzheimer's disease.

2.   Using the example you chose, compare what was first communicated to the public through the media with what was then said by health care providers. To determine what was communicated by the health care provider, try to read subsequent position statements by medical organizations on the topic, or reactions by health care providers who interpreted the media's message differently.

3.   Use an online search for a recent health update or breakthrough. Local newspapers, weekly magazines, and professional health journals are potential sources for initial and follow-up articles.

Communicating Health and Health Education Needs, Concerns, and Resources

Competency D
Foster communication between health care providers and consumers.

Sub-Competency 1
Identify the significance and implications of health care providers' messages to consumers.

Activity: Persuasive Communication

Student Outcome: The student can identify factors that influence an individual's acceptance of health information and services.

Directions:

1.   Obtain a copy of McGuire's (1984) article noted in "Getting Started." In it the author identifies five components and related variables of *persuasive communication*. These include variables related to the source, message, *channel*, receiver, and destination or outcome.

2.   Read the article and then identify three populations and health topics to be used in this activity. Specify the age, gender, race, socioeconomic status, and current knowledge level of the target population. An example population is middle-aged, minority, middle-class men enrolled in a cardiac rehabilitation program. The topic is stress management.

3.   For each identified population and topic, develop a health communication program which incorporates each of the components and related variables. Specifically you should identify:

   * Who will deliver your message?
   * What type of message will be delivered?
   * Through which channel will the message be delivered?
   * When will the message be delivered and how much information will be provided?

4.   Explain the reasoning underlying your choices.

Getting Started

McGuire, W. J. (1984). Public communication as a strategy for inducing health promoting behavior change. Preventive Medicine, 13, 299-313.

Communicating Health and Health Education Needs, Concerns, and Resources

Competency D
Foster communication between health care providers and consumers.

Sub-Competency 2
Act as a liaison between consumer groups and individuals and health care provider organizations.

Activity: A Letter To The Editor

Student Outcome: The student can translate key issues concerning access to health care as described in Healthy People 2000 for a general audience.

Directions:

1.   To complete this activity, you will need to obtain the full report of Healthy People 2000.

2.   Read and review Chapter 21 on Clinical Preventive Services (pp. 530-543). Summarize the key issues, problems, and concerns outlined in this chapter.

3.   Imagine that you are writing a letter to the editor of your local newspaper. Write the letter to inform the general public about the primary health care issues described in the reading.

4.   Remember you are summarizing the key issues. The entire letter should be no more than 300 words. Include the word count on your letter and submit it to your instructor.

Getting Started

U.S. Department of Health and Human Services. (1990). Healthy people 2000: National health promotion and disease prevention objectives (DHHS Publication No. PHS 91-50212). Washington, DC: U.S. Government Printing Office.

Communicating Health and Health Education Needs, Concerns, and Resources

Competency D
Foster communication between health care providers and consumers.

Sub-Competency 2
Act as a liaison between consumer groups and individuals and health care provider organizations.

<u>Activity:</u> <u>The Newspaper Article</u>

Student Outcome: The student can develop a newspaper article which will assist consumers in making better health care decisions.

Directions:

1. Select one of the consumer health topics listed below. If you are interested in a different consumer topic, check with your instructor to receive approval.

    a. Advantages and disadvantages of brand name vs. generic drugs
    b. Guidelines for selecting a physician or dentist
    c. Considerations when deciding whether or not to enter a hospice program
    d. Use of a chiropractor and other alternative healers
    e. Use of health maintenance organizations (HMO) and preferred provider organizations (PPO)

2. Gather information related to the consumer issue selected. (A search on the Internet will result in a number of sources of information on these topics.)

3. Develop and write an article for a college campus newspaper. Include all important information necessary for the reader to make an informed decision. Write no less than 200 words, but no more than 300. Next, using a readability formula or scale, determine the reading level of the campus newspaper. Then conduct a readability test on your article to see if its reading level is reasonably similar. If your article's readability score is too high or too low, adjust the number of polysyllabic words in your article. Include both a word count and the readability score on the article that you turn into the instructor. Attach a list of references used to complete this activity.

<u>Getting Started</u>

Locate a readability form or scale. If you have difficulty locating one, see Appendix B, "How to Test for Readability - The SMOG Readability Formula," pages 77-79, in the following source:

National Cancer Institute. (1992). <u>Making health communication programs work: A planner's guide.</u> (NIH Publication No. 92-1493/t068). Bethesda, MD: Author.

Notes

Glossary of Terms

behavioral psychology: one aspect of the psychology discipline which focuses on an individual's values, attitudes, and beliefs and the resultant influences on behavior

channel: the pathway or route for delivering a message

flier: promotional or advertising information, usually on 8½" x 11" paper, intended for circulation or posting in specified areas

flip chart: a series of pages that can be turned to display a sequence of information

graphic: relating to pictures or drawings in print format

ground rules: a set of regulations established by the facilitator and the group in order to encourage participation, maintain discipline, and respect the rights of all group members

liaison: one who establishes and maintains communication between two or more parties

marquee: a permanent public display board with messages that change periodically

mass media: organizations that develop and transmit messages that are received by large audiences, including various forms of printed materials and messages sent via the radio and television

model: design which serves as a guide for another to copy or imitate

persuasive communication: communication aimed at convincing individuals to process new information which encourages the adoption of healthful behaviors

press release: information provided in a standard format to news reporters and radio and television broadcasters for release to the public

public service announcement (PSA): reporting information to the public on radio or television without a charge by the media

social marketing: the process of adapting marketing principles and concepts in order to influence voluntary behavior change of target audiences to improve personal and societal health

target audience: a group of people who have been identified specifically for an educational intervention; generally, the group has specific characteristics in common

Notes

References

Downie, R. S., Fyfe, C., & Tannahill, A. (1990). Health promotion models and values. Oxford, England: Oxford University Press.

McGuire, W. J. (1984). Public communication as a strategy for inducing health promoting behavior change. Preventive Medicine, 13, 299-313.

National Cancer Institute. (1992). Making health communication programs work: A planner's guide. (NIH Publication No. 92-1493/t068). Bethesda, MD: Author.

National Commission for Health Education Credentialing, Inc. (1996). A competency-based framework for professional development of certified health education specialists. Allentown, PA: Author.

Ratzan, S. C. (1994). Communication–The key to a healthier tomorrow. American Behavioral Scientist, 38 (2), 202-207.

Roper, W. L. (1993). Health communication takes on new dimensions at CPC. Public Health Reports, 108 (2), 179-183.

Notes

Appendix

Responsibility I - Assessing Individual and Community Needs for Health Education

Competency A: Obtain health-related data about social and cultural environments, growth and development factors, needs and interests.

    Sub-Competency 1: Select valid sources of information about health needs and information.

    Sub-Competency 2: Utilize computerized sources of health-related information.

    Sub-Competency 3: Employ or develop appropriate data-gathering information.

    Sub-Competency 4: Apply survey techniques to acquire health data.

Competency B: Distinguish between behaviors that foster and those that hinder well-being.

    Sub-Competency 1: Investigate physical, social, emotional, and intellectual factors influencing health behaviors.

    Sub-Competency 2: Identify behaviors that tend to promote or compromise health.

    Sub-Competency 3: Recognize the role of learning and affective experiences in shaping patterns of health behavior.

Competency C: Infer needs for health education on the basis of obtained data.

    Sub-Competency 1: Examine needs assessment data.

    Sub-Competency 2: Determine priority areas of need for health education.

Responsibility II - Planning Effective Health Education Programs

Competency A: Recruit communication organizations, resource people, and potential participants for support and assistance in program planning.

    Sub-Competency 1: Communicate need for the program to those whose cooperation will be essential.

    Sub-Competency 2: Obtain commitment from personnel and decision makers who will be involved in the program.

    Sub-Competency 3: Seek ideas and opinions of those who will affect or be affected by the program.

    Sub-Competency 4: Incorporate feasible ideas and recommendations into the planning process.

Competency B: Develop a logical scope and sequence plan for a health
                     education program.

    Sub-Competency 1: Determine the range of health information requisite to a
                              given program of instruction.
    Sub-Competency 2: Organize the subject areas comprising the scope of a
                              program in logical sequence.

Competency C: Formulate appropriate and measurable program objectives.

    Sub-Competency 1: Infer educational objectives that facilitate achievement of
                              specified competencies.
    Sub-Competency 2: Develop a framework of broadly stated, operational
                              objectives relevant to a proposed health education
                              program.

Competency D: Design educational programs consistent with specified
                     program objectives.

    Sub-Competency 1: Match proposed learning activities with those implicit in
                              the stated objectives.
    Sub-Competency 2: Formulate a wide variety of alternative educational
                              methods.
    Sub-Competency 3: Select strategies best suited to implementation of
                              educational objectives in a given setting.
    Sub-Competency 4: Plan a sequence of learning opportunities building upon
                              and reinforcing mastery of preceding objectives.

Responsibility III - Implementing Health Education Programs

Competency A: Exhibit competence in carrying out planned programs.

    Sub-Competency 1: Employ a wide range of educational methods and
                              techniques.
    Sub-Competency 2: Apply individual or group process methods as appropriate
                              to given learning situations.
    Sub-Competency 3: Utilize instructional equipment and other instructional
                              media.
    Sub-Competency 4: Select methods that best facilitate practice of program
                              objectives.

Competency B: Infer enabling objectives as needed to implement instructional
                     programs in specified settings.

    Sub-Competency 1: Pretest learners to ascertain present abilities and
                              knowledge relative to proposed program objectives.
    Sub-Competency 2: Develop subordinate measurable objectives as needed for
                              instruction.

Competency C: Select methods and media best suited to implement program plans for specific learners.

    Sub-Competency 1: Analyze learner characteristics, legal aspects, feasibility, and other considerations influencing choices among methods.

    Sub-Competency 2: Evaluate the efficacy of alternative methods and techniques capable of facilitating program objectives.

    Sub-Competency 3: Determine the availability of information, personnel, time, and equipment needed to implement the program for a given audience.

Competency D: Monitor educational programs, adjusting objectives and activities as necessary.

    Sub-Competency 1: Compare actual program activities with the stated objectives.

    Sub-Competency 2: Assess the relevance of existing program objectives to current needs.

    Sub-Competency 3: Revise program activities and objectives as necessitated by changes in learner needs.

    Sub-Competency 4: Appraise applicability of resources and materials relative to given educational objectives.

Responsibility IV - *Evaluating Effectiveness of Health Education Programs*

Competency A: Develop plans to assess achievement of program objectives.

    Sub-Competency 1: Determine standards of performance to be applied as criteria of effectiveness.

    Sub-Competency 2: Establish a realistic scope of evaluation efforts.

    Sub-Competency 3: Develop an inventory of existing valid and reliable tests and instruments.

    Sub-Competency 4: Select appropriate methods for evaluating program effectiveness.

Competency B: Carry out evaluation plans.

    Sub-Competency 1: Facilitate administration of the tests and activities specified in the plan.

    Sub-Competency 2: Utilize data collection methods appropriate to the objectives.

    Sub-Competency 3: Analyze resulting evaluation data.

Competency C: Interpret results of program evaluation.

    Sub-Competency 1: Apply criteria of effectiveness to obtaining results of a program.

Sub-Competency 2: Translate evaluation results into terms easily understood by others.

Sub-Competency 3: Report effectiveness of educational programs in achieving proposed objectives.

Competency D: Infer implications from findings for future program planning.

Sub-Competency 1: Explore possible explanations for important evaluation findings.

Sub-Competency 2: Recommend strategies for implementing results of evaluation.

Responsibility V - *Coordinating Provision of Health Education Services*

Competency A: Develop a plan for coordinating health education services.

Sub-Competency 1: Determine the extent of available health education services.

Sub-Competency 2: Match health education services to proposed program activities.

Sub-Competency 3: Identify gaps and overlaps in the provision of collaborative health services.

Competency B: Facilitate cooperation between and among levels of program personnel.

Sub-Competency 1: Promote cooperation and feedback among personnel related to the program.

Sub-Competency 2: Apply various methods of conflict reduction as needed.

Sub-Competency 3: Analyze the role of health educator as liaison between program staff and outside groups and organizations.

Competency C: Formulate practical modes of collaboration among health agencies and organizations.

Sub-Competency 1: Stimulate development of cooperation among personnel responsible for community health education programs.

Sub-Competency 2: Suggest approaches for integrating health education within existing health programs.

Sub-Competency 3: Develop plans for promoting collaborative efforts among health agencies and organizations with mutual interests.

Competency D: Organize in-service training for teachers, volunteers, and other interested personnel.

Sub-Competency 1: Plan an operational, competency oriented training program.

Sub-Competency 2: Utilize instructional resources that meet a variety of in-service training needs.

Sub-Competency 3: Demonstrate a wide range of strategies for conducting in-service training programs.

Responsibility VI - Acting as a Resource Person in Health Education

Competency A: Utilize computerized health information retrieval systems effectively.

Sub-Competency 1: Match an information need with the appropriate retrieval system.

Sub-Competency 2: Access principal on-line and other database health information resources.

Competency B: Establish effective consultive relationships with those requesting assistance in solving health-related problems.

Sub-Competency 1: Analyze parameters of effective consultative relationships.

Sub-Competency 2: Describe special skills and abilities needed by health educators for consultation activities.

Sub-Competency 3: Formulate a plan for providing consultation to other health professionals.

Sub-Competency 4: Explain the process of marketing health education consultative services.

Competency C: Interpret and respond to requests for health information.

Sub-Competency 1: Analyze general processes for identifying the information needed to satisfy a request.

Sub-Competency 2: Employ a wide range of approaches in referring requesters to valid sources of health information.

Competency D: Select effective educational resource materials for dissemination.

Sub-Competency 1: Assemble educational material of value to the health of individuals and community groups.

Sub-Competency 2: Evaluate the worth and applicability of resource materials for given audiences.

Sub-Competency 3: Apply various processes in the acquisition of resource materials.

Sub-Competency 4: Compare different methods for distributing educational materials.

Responsibility VII - Communicating Health and Health Education Needs, Concerns, and Resources

Competency A: Interpret concepts, purposes, and theories of health education.

> **Sub-Competency 1:** Evaluate the state-of-the-art of health education.
> **Sub-Competency 2:** Analyze the foundations of the discipline of health education.
> **Sub-Competency 3:** Describe major responsibilities of the health educator in the practice of health education.

Competency B: Predict the impact of societal value systems on health education programs.

> **Sub-Competency 1:** Investigate social forces causing opposing viewpoints regarding health education needs and concerns.
> **Sub-Competency 2:** Employ a wide range of strategies for dealing with controversial health issues.

Competency C: Select a variety of communication methods and techniques in providing health information.

> **Sub-Competency 1:** Utilize a wide range of techniques for communicating health and health education information.
> **Sub-Competency 2:** Demonstrate proficiency in communicating health information and health education needs.

Competency D: Foster communication between health care providers and consumers.

> **Sub-Competency 1:** Identify the significance and implications of health care providers' messages to consumers.
> **Sub-Competency 2:** Act as liaison between consumer groups and individuals, and health care provider organizations.

Responsibilities adapted from:

National Commission for Health Education Credentialing, Inc. (1996). <u>A competency-based framework for professional development of certified health education specialists.</u> Allentown, PA: Author.